Equality in the Workplace

Human Resource Management in Action Series

Other HRM books from Blackwell Business

Equality in the Workplace

An Equal Opportunities Handbook for Trainers

Helen Collins

First published 1995

Blackwell Publishers, the publishing imprint of
Basil Blackwell Ltd
108 Cowley Road
Oxford OX4 1JF
UK

Basil Blackwell Inc.
238 Main Street
Cambridge, Massachusetts 02142
USA

British Library Cataloguing in Publication Data
A CIP catalogue record for this book is available from the British Library.

Library of Congress Cataloging-in-Publication Data
Collins, Helen.
    Equality in the workplace: an equal opportunities handbook for trainers
Helen Collins.
        p. cm.
    Includes index.
    ISBN 0-631-19393-6 (pbk. : alk. paper)
    1. Employees–Training of.   2. Minorities–Employment.   I. Title.   II. Series.
HF5549.5.T7C5897   1995
658.3'1245–dc20
                                                                94-22603
                                                                    CIP

Typeset in 11 on 13pt Plantin by Best-set Typesetter Ltd.
Printed in Great Britain by T. J. Press Ltd, Padstow, Cornwall

This book is printed on acid-free paper

Contents

Figures

Preface

Who is this Workbook for?

There is now an extensive range of literature covering most areas in the field of equal opportunities. However, there has not yet been any detailed study which has sought to consider the different initiatives concerned with training issues for employers and others. This handbook should fill that gap. It has been planned so as to enable readers to put it to a variety of uses, depending on their perspective and relationship to training activities concerning equal opportunities.

Many of those who have found themselves running equal opportunities training courses have never really planned to become trainers – they have more or less fallen or been thrown into the situation through the nature of their jobs in areas associated with equal opportunities or a high degree of personal concern. They come from a wide variety of backgrounds, many having had successful careers in other areas, not necessarily related to training. We learn from the insight and experience of others, and one of the things this workbook aims to do is to share experiences about all aspects of the training process.

If you are a provider of training it will:

- Inform you about the variety of issues that affect the quality and effectiveness of the training you may wish to provide
- Enable you to examine the training you may be undertaking with employees and others in order to assess how it is progressing
- Help you in considering and choosing appropriate training strategies and methods
- Inform you about the tasks, competencies and skills needed to carry out successful equal opportunities training

If you are a trainer or course facilitator it will:

- Enable you to develop an overview of all the areas and issues involved in equal opportunities training activities
- Help you to decide what training you can provide or would like to provide
- Assist you in choosing appropriate methods and focus for training
- Help you to consider the role that training has in your organization
- Enable you to assess the training you are offering or intend to offer
- Indicate areas of course content and design that you should consider in any training activities
- Help you to reassess any training you are already doing and plan for effective training related to needs and training requirements

For every reader it will:

- Provide an opportunity to share the process of training that providers of equal opportunities training have been struggling with over the last few years
- Enable you to get some sense of the range of experiences of others and how they operate so that you can get some ideas on how to tackle your own issues
- Provide frameworks and reference points, background material and sources of information to help assess your training activities or training needs
- Enable you to see patterns to prompt your thinking about the area, so that you will cover all the important areas and not leave anything crucial out of account

Abbreviations

ACAS	Advisory, Conciliation and Arbitration Service
AIDS	Acquired Immune Deficiency Syndrome
AIMS	Association for Improvements in the Maternity Services
BACIE	British Association for Commercial and Industrial Education
BAECE	British Association for Early Childhood Education
BCODP	British Council of Organizations of Disabled People
BPW	Business and Professional Women
BTEC	Business and Technology Education Council
CBI	Confederation of British Industry
CEDP	Committees for the Employment of Disabled People
CHE	Campaign for Homosexual Equality
CRE	Commission for Racial Equality
EOC	Equal Opportunities Commission
EWC	Expected Week of Confinement
EWMDN	European Women's Management Development Network
FREE	Forum on the Rights of the Elderly to Education
GLF	Gay Liberation Front
GOQ	Genuine Occupational Qualification
HEA	Health Education Authority
HIV	Human Immunodeficiency Virus
IPM	Institute of Personnel Management
IT	Industrial Tribunal
ITD	Institute of Training and Development
LAGER	Lesbian and Gay Employment Rights
LEA	Local Education Authority
LEC	Local Enterprise Company

NACRO	National Association for the Care and Resettlement of Offenders
NANFC	National Association of Nursery and Family Care
NCT	National Childbirth Trust
NCVCO	National Council of Voluntary Childcare
NCVQ	National Council for Vocational Qualifications
NI	National Insurance
PACT	Placing, Assessment and Counselling Team
PANN	Professional Association of Nursery Nurses
PPA	Pre-school Play Groups Association
PRA	Pre-Retirement Association
QW	Qualifying Week
RADAR	The Royal Association for Disability and Rehabilitation
REC	Racial Equality Council
ROW	Rights of Women
RRA	Race Relations Act
RREAS	Race Relations Employment Advisory Service
SCAFA	Scottish Child and Family Alliance
SDA	Sex Discrimination Act
SIACE	Scottish Institute of Adult and Continuing Education
SMP	Statutory Maternity Pay
TDLB	Training and Development Lead Body
TEC	Training and Enterprise Council
TEED	Training, Enterprise and Education Directorate
TNA	Training Needs Audit/Analysis
VOLCUF	Voluntary Organizations Liaison Council for Under Fives
WASH	Women Against Sexual Harassment
WLM	Women's Liberation Movement

1 Introduction
Training: Trends and Current Issues

It can be stated unequivocally that in any organization training is nothing other than a means of survival in an extremely competitive and rapidly changing environment. Staff are the key factor and determine the success of any large-scale project. The importance of this human factor cannot be overemphasized for innovation or the widening of horizons; it is in this mode that training must be incorporated into a company strategy and into the day-to-day activities of as many organizations as possible. All such measures to promote training are thus deliberately multifaceted and should form part of an ongoing process. The extreme usefulness of equal opportunities training should not be ignored since it brings to a firm a new outlook and enthusiasm.

Several evolutions have had an impact on training in the last decade. Technological evolutions, social and political changes and the internationalization of markets are rendering organizational management and planning increasingly difficult. Change and evolution go hand in hand with uncertainty, the inability to plan and unpredictability. Training ensures that a workforce has the ability to reach and maintain a leading position; equal opportunities training ensures that employee and organizational status is continuously enhanced and not held back by discriminatory forces.

Hardly a government speech is complete nowadays without a ritual mention of the role training is to play in the renewal of economic prosperity. Captains of industry, think tanks and a variety of public bodies eagerly echo the same theme – not surprisingly, because it sits neatly in any speech between the stirring words about the sacrifices needed in the battle against inflation and the conclusion about fruits of victory in terms of steady growth, full employment and increased economic wealth. Too rarely, however, does the theme of training stretch to a full speech. That is because there appear to be no simple solutions to a host of awkward questions about who is to meet the costs of training and how the rewards of improved training will be shared between the sponsor, the trainee and the taxpayer. Without answers to these questions, or at least better answers than we have currently got, it is difficult to see training objectives as anything other than a wish list. Training activity becomes at best good citizenry rather than the engine of growth it is supposed to be. Equality is about changing people's prejudices to render the release of increased potential in every member of a workforce. This increase can be realized and profitably utilized without vast investment in capital – by breaking down the barriers of prejudice that serve ultimately as obstacles to organizational progress through equal opportunities training.

One of the reasons for the traditional fuzziness surrounding equal opportunities training plans is that few in positions of authority and influence dare take formal responsibility for the training agenda. It is easy to appreciate how difficult and unscientific any human resource planning exercise is and therefore leaving the market to sort things out is at least an option, albeit a short-sighted one doomed to failure. Training has often been regarded as secondary to the importance of putting the right people in charge. As a result, one area that has received huge injections of expense is the upper managerial echelons, both in state and private organizations. The uninitiated might think that this massive effort would have transformed the supply of competent professional managers. Surprisingly this does not seem to have happened; instead, spectacular pay increases for senior managers have been justified by the extreme difficulty in getting the right people, while the companies paying these salaries do not seem to have enjoyed much improvement in performance. Greater attention to equality in the workplace might have ensured that people reached their maximum potential without enormous investment.

Training: a Make or Buy Decision?

If training needs have to be left to the market it follows that employers, particularly private sector employers, are calling the shots. To them, training is another make or buy decision, where building a skilled workforce through training and development is one alternative and buying it in ready made from the external labour market is the other. Filling staff vacancies through training and internal development, however, takes a long time and also means the company needs some sort of personnel plan, underpinned by an effective equal opportunities programme that makes full use of each employee's effectiveness.

Given the uncertainties involved in training for specific future human resource needs it is easy to understand why training managers are now tending to emphasize skills training where workforces can be drilled with a set of procedures that create simple but robust payoffs in virtually all circumstances. Many large companies now provide open learning centres where employees can access the latest materials on a self-study basis rather than through traditional courses. Equal opportunities training which consists of an instruction package involving the acquisition of specific skills and knowledge is increasingly being overtaken by interactive video and practical-based learning. If courses are required it is often the outside agency, spreading the high costs of training across a large customer base, that is the cheapest source. The move out of house gathers momentum. This is partly because in many companies the in-house training function has been made a profit centre which proves uncompetitive because it has been saddled with the responsibility for maintaining some crumbling Victorian pile bought by the company in a previous burst of prosperity.

But whether training is in-house or outsourced there is no doubt that relying entirely on organizationally based training is bad news. Just as some line managers might be tempted to tear down any internal vacancy notices on the grounds that they tempt away his or her best staff, so they will do their best to discourage their staff to train, because if they do, not only will there be the cost of the absence it entails but the trainee may expect a pay increase and probably a career move. The organization may benefit, but the managers who lose their best staff members see few plus points. But with equal opportunities training, everyone benefits, both in humanitarian and economic terms. Apart from traditional approaches to training, many organizations are therefore introducing a range of specific equality measures to ensure that various equality programmes are continuously improved, for the benefit of the organization and employees alike.

Training providers have moved to alter the balance of advantage by offering more for less. They know training is about providing people with the techniques, understanding and structure to solve their own problems. Unfortunately this takes rather a long time and seems to cost rather more than the market will bear. Rather conveniently, high levels of comprehension among many trainees has allowed them to telescope training into half or less of the time it would have taken a decade ago. However, society tends to get parts replacers rather than fully skilled workers at the end of this process. And with equality training, a little knowledge can be a dangerous thing, as the benefits to be gained risk being lost in the isolation and separation of one discriminator from another, thus producing only part-equality.

Training: Compliance or Deviance?

The strategic aim of a good training programme should not be to produce a set of efficiently programmed and motivated clones with competence certificates and BS validation. What most organizations, particularly UK organizations, need are a few more innovators or dropouts who challenge the system, and see new uses for resources and opportunities in a novel and unexpected way. If we had a boom economy handling major change successfully then replicating the formula as widely as possible to bring the good up to the standard of the best may have some justification. But the needs of an economy which generates too few new businesses, too few jobs and generally too few ideas hardly needs training predicated on the status quo. Instead we need training to generate a few more innovators. It is the innovators who change things. Providing a platform based on full equality is the best way to motivate staff to test out their ideas and potential to the benefit of themselves and their organizations. We have, however, made it so much harder for them to do so because now they need not just an idea but also the confidence and skills to battle their way through the regiments of well-trained managers and other officials who will always be able to think of a reason why something shouldn't happen. Equal opportunities provision stimulates at the very least an awareness of maximized potential and at most a realization of maximized potential.

Change and the Changing Skill of the Human Resource Professional

Where training was mainly an exclusive answer to change, it is now increasingly used to guide the process(es) of change, to monitor change and to prepare people for continuous evolution. Since 1980 the pattern in many firms has consisted of:

• a dramatic stiffening of competitive environment;
• a loss of competitive advantage;
• rapid changes in business strategy and structure;
• changes in employment levels.

A complex set of business environment changes have led to a series of generic, strategic responses. The following six, often interdependent, responses have driven human resource development:

• internationalization;
• competitive restructuring;
• decentralization;
• acquisitions and mergers;
• total quality processes;
• technological change.

These business responses have in turn triggered action in a range of human resource areas:

• human resource development;
• effecting organizational and cultural changes;
• skill supply;
• training and retraining;
• work organization and systems changes;
• selection, appraisal and retention;
• employee relations and compensation;
• managing outflows of people.

The overall pattern of change has been a reactive one, with human resource change following rather than leading or running in close association with business and technical change. Put simply and generally, competitive pressures lead to the perception of a business performance gap. Firms have generally responded to this gap in two ways. First, the development of their products and their market position. Second, technical change within the organization. These responses were made singly or together, and in turn led to a further perception of a skills performance gap.

The human resource issues triggered by business and technical change are complex and highly interrelated and challenge the firm across short, medium and long term perspectives. Few of the issues can be tackled by pulling one human resource lever, be it training, recruitment, or compensation. The distinction between 'driving and stabilizing' forces is an important one for understanding a firm's capacity for generating training activity. While the initial trigger may be product market development or technical change, other factors also need to be present to achieve effective and sustainable activity in training. The factors involved fall into four categories:

- business/strategic;
- the external/internal labour markets;
- internal actors, training systems, philosophy and management organization;
- external training stimuli and support, including funding.

The propensity to train is generally enhanced where an efficient combination of the above forces apply. By the same token, decay or inertia in training activity is the result of a decline in one or more of these forces, along with additional, specifically negative factors.

Mobilizing for Change

There are a great many factors which influence the extent of a firm's training. The point is that no single one by itself is sufficient – effective sustainable activity in training requires a rich array of influences which have to be built up additively in a way that links to features of local organizational contexts as well as management processes.

Mobilizing training is often a question of internal politics and key personalities and a building up of activities well linked to the business and exploiting openings created by subsequent product market and technical changes. The initiation of any new training or development usually starts a 'learning by doing' process, creating opportunities to generate activities at various organizational levels and building multiple pressure points for future more carefully focused expenditure.

Effective change (towards high levels of training) can therefore be seen as resulting from a mobilization of positive factors, and neutralization of negative ones. What distinguishes one firm from another is the extent to which the key 'actors' have created a supportive context for training and development activity. And no context epitomizes this more than in a firm's willingness and ability to embody a corporate equality ethos through an ongoing equal opportunities programme. The management issue is, therefore, the need to build a receptive context in advance. Once that has been achieved training activity is more likely to build up incrementally even if at first it is decidedly *ad hoc*. In time evidence of training 'successes' will accrue, contributing to a still more favourable context for future activity. When this is properly linked to business developments a positive spiral is established.

Expanding the Horizons of Human Resource Management

A number of discernible trends point to a need for a reorientation of the human resource function, and a reorientation of directors and line managers towards human resource activity. Mass redundancies and interrelated skill changes have occurred and are continuing to occur which are not solvable by single means. Technological and product market changes directly affecting one group have knock-on effects that need to be managed by forward thinking. Human resource studies have found substantial evidence of skill change, driven ultimately by competitive pressure, as an underlying imperative. This has been accompanied by a shift in the priorities and focus of the human resource function away from industrial relations problems towards training and development in the cause of upgrading skills. The two activities are different, in that industrial relations is about 'defending' the organization while training and management development is about 'advancing' them. The latter activity brings the human resource professional much closer to business strategy.

High levels of training in an organization are more likely where there is a philosophy of continuous development, and a desire to magnify employee usefulness by providing a workforce with equality of opportunity. A workable policy of continuous development means attention to a range of human resource levers. In this sense the training has to nest within human resource development. Coordinated activity of this kind, underpinned by a set of values that favours the development of people, is a central human resource development tenet.

Further pressures for change are emerging from demographic and international pressures. Changes in the structure of markets, particularly from the effects of the single European market, will have wide unforeseeable impacts on skills and attitudes, and hasten the pace for change. The management of change has become a prime preoccupation of senior management. The increased complexity of the internal and external environment and the magnitude of change that organizations have had to cope with mean that any change is likely to be a complex process. Apart from the need to equip managers with the breadth of perspective to address this, managing cultural transition is an important, though underrated task.

The Need for New Human Resource Skills and Knowledge

The above pressures and opportunities signify a need for human resource professionals, including training professionals, to acquire new skills and knowledge. The first of these areas of skills and knowledge relates to the development of broad training and experience across the full range of human resource activities. Harvard Business School research has conceptualized human resource management activity into four broad terms:

* human resource flows;
* work systems;
* rewards systems;
* employee relations.

These are some of the critical areas of training and development for human resource professionals, and underpinning each is the concept of equality, and the consequent benefits in terms of increased staff motivation, high morale, greater productivity and innovation. The notion of human resource covers recruitment and selection, training and development, equal opportunities, counselling and appraisal, career and succession planning, and is bound by personnel planning processes. The separate specification of 'work systems' draws attention to a level of technical knowledge which is often not recognized in human resource work as always present. The distinct characterization of reward systems reflects the specialist status the management of pay or compensation systems have in many large organizations. Both the latter, however, are intimately related to elements in human resource flow processes. Employee relations signifies the greater emphasis on positive policies like communications and consultation, rather than the defensive overtones of 'industrial relations'. While there has undoubtedly been a shift in the skills employed in this area in the UK, traditional industrial relations skills in bargaining remain highly valued.

A second major area of training and development for human resource professionals relates to their ability to think in business and human resource management terms. This involves:

- Conceptual thinking founded on a sound appreciation of changing business and human resource needs and on the interconnection between the two (including the impact of international processes).
- Diagnostic skills to audit, or to take stock of, the inheritance of skills in the light of actual or likely business and technological changes.
- The ability to respond and be market or need driven, recognizing that it is often necessary first to sort out the business and organization structure.
- The ability to recognize a changing business situation, to adjust services and practices in anticipation, and to initiate a new style of human resource management. This may involve a broader set of linked human resource activities, as when an organization grows by a reliance on recruitment and its consequent need to give attention to training and career development.
- The ability to identify and advise on business opportunities afforded by the strength of the skill base, thereby translating human resources into a perceived source of competitive advantage.

It is critical for human resource professionals to acquire a range of skills if they seek to implement equal opportunities in a firm. These process skills include the following strategic and technical skills:

- the ability to diagnose receptive and non-receptive contexts for equal opportunities activity, and the political skills to mobilize internal and external forces to facilitate such activity;
- the ability to recognize and exploit a wide range of pressure points for change, to build positive spirals of action;

- sensitivity to the changing internal situation during a major change programme, and the ability to initiate timely adjustments and agreements in equal opportunities practices;
- recognizing the role of 'learning by doing' in the development of equal opportunities strategy and training activity;
- involvement in managing the evolution of the equality culture by finding the right balance between recruitment and training and development, and by the blending of old and new staff in appointments and promotions.

Such culture change processes are often critical for the success of both business and human resource changes. Any process needs to be carried out in such a way that it meets new task requirements while being sensitive to individual job satisfaction and career aspirations, and preserving what is valuable from previous missions and values. Successful transition is a matter of:

- promoting, controlling the pace of, and stabilizing cultural change;
- managing and motivating people through the implementation and continuous development of equality measures.

The Strategic Role of the Training Manager

It has been argued above that the institutionalization of training is much more likely to occur where training is itself part of a broader process of human resource thinking and action. Such broader processes of human resource development are unlikely to occur if the people factor is not connected with the critical pathway of a business. If an equal opportunities training manager is to acquire a more strategic role, that would clearly need to link those broader processes with the critical path of the business and also the wider thinking about human resource development going on in an organization. Where this has occurred it has been underpinned by a number of factors:

- the strong championing of equal opportunities at the highest level in an organization;
- a strong devolution of equal opportunities matters down the line of the organization in such a way that equality factors are integrated into the line managers' customary preoccupation with business matters;

• an equality function which is itself well connected with the line management system and is working on problems that the line management system feels to be critical for the competitive success of the firm.

Many equal opportunities functions are now being led by senior line managers with the human resource director post being a critical learning post for fast track line managers. In this context, a highly expert group of specialist human resource professionals with skills in all equality functions is critical. These skills include the ability to:

• analyse a firm's current equality ethos;
• analyse a firm's potential to implement and improve upon equality practices;
• set realistic targets such as positive action programmes;
• monitor an equal opportunities programme;
• evaluate an equal opportunities programme;
• keep abreast of European, UK and local equality matters including legislation, campaigns, networks and other developments.

The process requirements for the human resource function here may be to give up the fragmentation and overspecialization of the past and to organize personnel work in a much more task-related and network-based fashion.

To the equal opportunities training specialist part of this network, there are great opportunities if the trainer has conceptual and practical skills in order to link thinking about business change to some of a firm's critical management tasks and a diagnosis of critical training and development needs. Finding pathways and processes to link line managers and other human resource professionals into a diagnosis about business strategy change, critical management tasks and key training and development needs is a very important requirement for specifying training and developments for the future. It is also a critical way of building up the commitment of line managers who need to continue to take equality training and development matters seriously as a business tool.

Part I
The Trainer and the Organization

2
Organizing and Managing Equal Opportunities Training

Organizations are not only integrating the equality dimension in their processes; as a result of many other changes greater demands are being placed on the competence of each individual employee. These changes include:

- internationalization and increased mobility;
- technological evolution, new technology and innovation;
- questions of quality;
- health and safety issues;
- flexibility;
- training;
- leisure.

Lifelong learning is the keyword for all levels of personnel within an organization. The development of human potential is leading to changes in the traditional boundaries between different segments of an organization, which will bring about changing organizational structures. This restructuring is changing the requirements of what employees are expected to contribute. New conditions call for increased:

- responsibility;
- loyalty;
- reliability;
- motivation;
- readiness to learn continuously.

Human qualities are more important in the enterprise of today. Training is often used to motivate and to develop human resources within an organization. An optimal development of human resources should make two major contributions:

• the achievement of collective/corporate objectives;
• the self-development of the employee.

Training in this sense cannot only be linked to the technical functioning of the production process, but to the better functioning of the organization as an environment where opportunities to learn are optimized. But most of all, training is used as a response to the gap between the competences that an individual has (available competences), and the competences that an organization requires.

The extent to which there is an overlap between the required and the available competences determines the way in which a person is able to carry out the tasks required by an organization. When changes take place relatively slowly, it is possible to adapt the available competences to the required ones with a singular or limited number of specific training actions. If changes take place quickly, as they have recently, continuous training is required.

Recent changes tend towards a position where more emphasis is put on a variety of new factors such as:

• non-routine work capacities;
• individual responsibility;
• group work;
• interactive work;
• initiative taking;
• problem identification, analysis and problem solving;
• networking.

These evolutions will have an influence on the competences that trainers have to transfer and consequently have to possess.

One of the tasks of a training manager is to develop a grid with activities, tasks and competences for vocational trainers. The starting point is a scheme with activities related to the following stages:

• training needs analysis;
• conception of a training programme, which is a translation of the results of the training needs analysis in terms of training;
• establishment of an operational plan;
• implementation of an operational plan;
• evaluation.

Each of these stages is linked with tasks which require competences. In turn, the tasks can be regrouped into functions in the field of training.

Trainers cannot escape from the organizational context in which they work. Even the start of a programme is marked by the attitudes and views the participants bring with them from a variety of sources including:

- their sections or departments;
- their colleagues and friends;
- their private lives;
- their past experiences about the relevance of training to themselves and their jobs;
- their concerns and issues generated by the environment in which they work.

These may have little to do with the training programme arranged for them and as a result not everyone will be keenly awaiting a creative and imaginative training programme. Their receptiveness to the training may well be affected by factors that an experienced and prepared trainer would have made it their business to consider and if possible influence in some way. Yet many equal opportunities trainers, and indeed trainers in general, are not organization people. By the very nature of their work, they will tend to be relatively autonomous and individualistic in their work patterns. There are, however, considerable gains to be made by the trainers who appreciate, empathize and take full account of the organizational context and culture in which they work. It can be extremely helpful for any trainer to have an overview of the organization in which he or she is planning to stage an equality programme, and in particular the role and functioning of training.

Strategies and Policies: their Importance for Training

Developing an equal opportunities training policy and strategy for an organization can often appear far less attractive than undertaking other activities. For someone new in a post it can also seem very daunting and can tend to be put off until later. But a really successful training response cannot be handled appropriately without something that can be called a policy, review or strategy. If a training programme's content is to be closely related to organizational needs, it follows that it is difficult to carry it out without clear statements of intent by an organization. It is also very difficult to determine training needs or to carry out training related to working environments and workers' needs without very well-defined strategies, policies and guidelines. Such guidelines form the training response's public face and the basis of the commitment of all the other departments and personnel. The strategy document produced does not have to be rigid and inflexible, it can indeed be quite the opposite. Yet it must indicate the philosophy, planning, aims and direction of the training response to equal opportunities.

In many instances equal opportunities training activities are taking place in a vacuum, and considering the importance many organizations nowadays attach to strategies and policies the existence of policy statements is not as widespread as might be expected. But if there is no strategy, nor even a policy to support such training or give a sense of direction and purpose, an organization has not fully validated the training. It is as if it does not really exist, is not considered important, or is regarded as a marginal issue. It can well be argued that the very nature of the work around equal opportunities means that there is all the more reason for having policies and strategies. Policies help to confront or solve several other key issues, for example:

- it is sometimes hard for trainers to feel visible in an organization; policies are one way to do something about it as it places the trainer and his or her activities clearly on an organization's agenda;
- written policies may also help in relations and negotiations with others, for once adopted it in effect makes the whole organization, not just the individual trainer, responsible for the training;
- policies can be used to influence or shape managers' action plans, budgets, resources and energy.

Producing a comprehensive policy and a training strategy on equal opportunities is not impossible. Some organizations have early on developed excellent and comprehensive policy statements with clear indications of carrying out extensive training programmes for all staff. The policy statement should strive to do four things:

- define an organization's position;
- identify general training needs;

- set guidelines on fitting training into other activities;
- provide a framework for detailed planning of a training programme including timing, client groups and equality targets to be met.

The training strategy should:

- define the relationship between the organization and the training needs;
- set realistic objectives and goals;
- provide guidelines for managers and others for planning and implementation;
- provide information for employees and give some indication of plans, scope and methods of training;
- say what will be expected to happen, making it clear where responsibilities for all parts of the programme lie.

The strategy is the public face of a training initiative and as such is the 'public relations' document for equal opportunities training. However, it is not only this aspect that makes a policy and strategy important for the trainer. It can also have considerable effects on the training itself. Training that takes place without this support often leaves the trainers with difficulties in handling queries and concerns, especially those related to actual working practices.

The following questions are designed to assist in developing a training policy and strategy on equal opportunities training:

- Are you clear what is a policy statement and a training strategy?
- Have you examined other policies and strategies?
- Have you spoken to other trainers in the organization or elsewhere about their ideas?
- Have you outlined a framework?
- Have you spoken to other people: managers, trade unions, equal opportunities representatives?
- Have you arranged to incorporate their views in the strategy?
- Is the policy/strategy flexible enough to handle most situations?
- Does the strategy complement the policy?
- Are there general statements or specific points?
- Have you made reference to delivery, resources, responsibilities, goals, objectives, outcomes, monitoring, review and evaluation?
- What arrangements do you have for reviews and modifications?

If you do not have or do not need a strategy or policy statement:

- Do you have some method of making your goals and objectives clear to others?

- Do you have some way of acquainting yourself with the views and expectations of others, particularly managers?
- Can you insert some references or key points about the training programme into other documents – staff newsletters, journals, notice boards, for instance?
- Can you ensure that you provide regular verbal feedback and receive verbal responses about the progress of a training programme from top managers?
- Have you explored other ways of communicating or negotiating with different parts of an organization?
- Have you made any attempts to share your plans and ideas informally, through the grapevine, for instance, or through another more formal network?

The Organizational Environment: the Influence of Culture and Change

One of the main issues facing many staff in large organizations today is the climate of change in which they operate and the degree of uncertainty that it generates at all levels. Today's large organization, medium-sized business, public or private body, is no longer a static or solid entity. It is shifting and changing, almost weekly, in response to several issues such as:

- government requirements;
- EU legislation and political pressures;
- labour market changes;
- the impact of new technology;
- changes in training and qualifications criteria.

Organizations can develop specific ways of responding to external events, and trainers can often find themselves having to deal with customs or behaviour they may never have dreamed would come their way. It is important to understand this when planning a training event and not to assume that what worked well in one organization will necessarily be welcomed in another. In the planning stage the context in which the training is taking place is as important as the training. In many cases the effectiveness and success of the training can be more dependent on effective planning than on a trainer's ability, knowledge and expertise in the field of equal opportunities.

It is not an easy task to provide advice about how to handle the environment and culture of any organization. It may be better posed as a series of questions for trainers to ask themselves, for example:

- Have you ever considered the culture of the organization in which you have trained or plan to train in the future? (It can be found in the activity patterns, interactions, values, attitudes, customs and procedures; it can be formal and visible or informal and invisible.)
- What is your own work environment like? If your section is sheltered and hidden, what do you really know about the work environment of others around you?
- Have you considered that the way your participants respond may be influenced by the chaotic culture and the many changes going on around them?
- What do you know about those changes? Have you found out about them so that you can be aware of their potential impact?
- How far are you aware of, and how far do you work with, both informal and formal aspects of the organization?
- Have you a sufficiently wide view about yourself and your training activities and where they fit in as well as what they may conflict with or oppose?

Using this section along with the key issues listed below should enable some of the more vague or elusive aspects of organizational behaviour to be recognized and worked with, rather than opposed and fought against.

Key points

- What do you understand by culture and environment?
- How are you going to find out more about this?
- Are there any key people who could help you understand more of what goes on in an organization?
- Do you have a perspective on the whole organization as well as the specific departments or personnel with whom you are working, the corporate view and the sectional?
- Do you take into consideration other key employment policies and their relationship to your work as well as their influence on participants' beliefs and behaviour?
- How much do you know about the general and specific pressures under which people you train work?
- Do you take time to try to understand the organization with which you are working and to familiarize yourself with the changes it has undergone?

The Training Function: Attitudes and Perceptions of Training

In general the role of training within many organizations has been towards the passive course provider mode, responding to crises, needs and requests. It is only since the early 1990s that it is slowly, and in some cases painfully, moving towards a training and development model that is more proactive within a framework similar to a consultancy model.

There is of course no single way of doing it, and some of the appeal of training lies in the amount of personal choice the trainer has, though he or she is affected by what role an organization allows its staff. An equal opportunities trainer's role should change over time and in different contexts. There is more to a training role than running courses. Even if a trainer feels more comfortable with this limited role, he or she should consider other options and take on new tasks and confront similar issues from different angles.

For anyone embarking on equal opportunities training there is much to consider in relation to what is meant by training. The obvious direct training/course provider approach may not be the most appropriate, nor may it be the most prevailing ethos in an organization in regard to training. The debate about what training should be held, along with any course responses or evaluations that are being made, automatically reflects the varied and complex nature of each organization and makes it imperative that these issues are given some credence. They will influence not only the speed, form and effectiveness of a training programme but also provide a basis for a wider training brief for future equal opportunities requirements.

Key considerations

- What is meant by training in your organization?
- Have you thought about other aspects of the training function you could take on board?
- Is there a good balance and a wide range of activities?
- What is the level of support for equal opportunities training in the organization?
- What is the degree of management involvement and support?
- Have you thought about investigating what others think your role should be?
- Are you falling into the trap of others' perceptions of your role?

The Location of Training

All organizations consist of systems, structures and hierarchies that can be dissected and analysed. More important than this though is how an organization utilizes those structures and the behaviour that results. When considering equal opportunities training activities there may be a logical response that can be made in respect of its location. However, because each organization has its own characteristics, structures and systems, there is often little rational cohesiveness lying behind the location of these new areas of work. Instead it can often appear eccentric and superficial rather than integrated, formal and comprehensive. The personnel appointed to carry out the range of equal opportunities activities can be viewed as assets for an organization to use creatively and flexibly, linking them into new service options. The narrower view is that they are just posts or tasks and belong to a department or section. Yet they are rare commodities in many organizations, so that deploying people's skills, ideas and expertise as widely as possible should at all times be encouraged, not discouraged.

The majority of large organizations are characterized by a number of features including:

- formal bureaucracies of hierarchy;
- huge amounts of paperwork relating to company rules, procedures, plans, personnel data, to name just a few;
- committees based on subject, departmental or rank specializations;
- strong departmentalization.

Such features can sometimes lead to inertia and a general difficulty in gaining responses. New equal opportunities posts, continuously being created, are supposed to be dynamic and responsive, but the individuals in them can often find themselves hamstrung by their place in the organization which circumscribes all their plans and activities.

The ways in which many firms organize themselves do not always help those working within their boundaries. Organizations are often unable to move quickly and creatively, and in fact can discourage innovation and risk taking. The present climate of constant change should have the opposite effect, but this is not the way many within organizational structures experience the changes.

The multiple departmental structures need not be restrictive. They should be able to be adaptive, but because of the way power and responsibility is often handled by managers and others the potential for autonomy does not always become the reality. These issues and problems are frequently brought into sharper prominence in training. The location of the trainer within an organization can influence the way in which he or she can respond to training needs and affect their success. The different focus and responsibilities of each section can be reflected in the quality and degree of work that trainers can undertake.

Many different disciplines and sections are involved in some way or another in equal opportunities training activities. Sometimes it is one department only, but often several can be found operating at the same time, with or without the knowledge of others. Responsibility for training may need to be taken at the executive level, rather than its location being dependent on a manager in a department who seizes the initiative and acts first. On the whole many organizations have devolved much of the responsibility for equal opportunities to human resource managers or sections.

There are three important trends or issues in relation to the location of training that can be found in many organizations tackling equal opportunities programmes:

- the separation that can occur between training activities and the responsibility for equal opportunities in the organization;
- the question of department versus corporate approaches;
- the low involvement of existing training specialists.

It is not uncommon to find that the training is taking place in a quite different area from that where authority and responsibility for equal opportunity activity lies. This results in variable quality of work and some confusion on the part of both trainers and participants.

A more planned, strategic and corporate approach to equal opportunities training is more likely to ensure that problems are minimized. Access can be easier but influencing the directions and activities of departments can be hard. While the different sections can acknowledge the centrality of the corporate approach, they can also pay lip service only and take very little real notice of events, or only as much as suits them. The trainer in a central location can therefore find that it is all responsibility with very little authority.

Among many equal opportunities trainers and specialists there is no common viewpoint on the most appropriate location for their workbase, though there are strong preferences for a corporate centralized function to pick up and coordinate all equal opportunities activities under the direction of a coordinator or adviser who has sufficient status and power to gain access to the most senior levels of an organization and the decision-making processes. Many organizations are now trying to grasp the issue of corporate responses and strategies, as some of the fragmentation and competitiveness between various sections is inappropriate in the present climate. However, old habits die hard and in an era of shrinking resources, departments tend to take whatever slice of the cake is on offer, and equal opportunities work is one of the few new areas open to development. If its focus lies initially in one or more departments then someone must make sure that it also spreads outwards to encompass other sections throughout the whole of the organization.

There is another gap in departmental links in that where they exist, there do not appear to be very strong links with any of the equal opportunities personnel. Many organizations now have staff with this as their prime responsibility. There can be links through employees working on women's issues, black and ethnic minority areas, HIV and AIDS in the workplace. The trainers too can make strenuous attempts to ensure that there is an equality perspective in all their courses as discrimination and prejudice – the bread and butter of equality work – are constantly present in equal opportunities work irrespective of its theme or location.

A corporate or centrally based location raises issues such as:

- no one department contributes
- uneven spread of involvement and competence, expertise and interest
- difficulties getting into departments
- need to have suitable level of status to influence
- hard to get corporate view from departments

Separated or departmentalized locations raise issues such as:

- weak knowledge of organization as a whole
- different approaches within different departments
- difficult to coordinate
- varying expertise of staff
- varying equality backgrounds among staff

Training organized by and located in established training sections raises issues such as:

- hold training expertise for organization, can fit into strategy
- may need to build up expertise
- often heavy workloads
- reputation and perception of past training programmes can affect the new work

Any organization thinking of expanding their equal opportunities work or employing equal opportunities specialists may find it helpful to consider these issues and locate the staff in an appropriate and planned setting.

Key points

- Where have you located equal opportunities specialist posts and equal opportunities trainers?
- Are they both in the same department or separate?
- What are the advantages and disadvantages of your choice of location?
- If there is some degree of separation of functions, how well do the various sections communicate with each other?
- Is there a common strategy or set of aims they all adhere to?
- If different departments are doing training, how is it coordinated and are consistency of quality and of content maintained?
- What role, if any, do the specialist training sections play in supporting equal opportunities training and related activities?
- If the training is department-based, how far is this affecting what the training is offering?
- Is one department doing training for another? How far is the expertise being shared?
- If one department is leading on the training, is it possible to share some of the training support activities with other sections?

The Role of Managers in Equal Opportunities Training

The primary role that managers play in relation to all training activities is highlighted in almost every instance where equal opportunities training is taking place or being planned. Successful and effective training programmes can only be fully successful where management teams accept their responsibility for the training and for its eventual outcomes. Training should be linked into organizational objectives, and therefore the ownership of any training programme properly belongs with the management as the representatives of the corporate organization. So it is not dogmatic to assert that managers must take personal responsibility for the training and development of their staff: it is the foundation on which any training programme can stand or fall. Often the very uncertainty that pervades the equal opportunities area is used as an excuse to put off formulating active management responses. Those managers who do take equal opportunities seriously enough to plan it into their priorities tend to stand out amidst the general discontent expressed by many in the field at the lack of interest and support.

Management involvement is also influenced by the various dynamics at play within an organization's structure. Trainers need to be aware of these, as they can sometimes cancel out perceived support, especially when the training often has to work across departmental and sectional divides. Any planning for training should therefore be very careful to take account of the various managerial cultures and interplays that could impinge on its effectiveness. Work done by those undertaking training with managers to create an awareness of their role and responsibilities must be worth the time and effort. It should foster in the managers an active interest in their staff's needs in relation to equal opportunities so that they can become actively involved in using opportunities that arise to improve and extend their staff's skills and knowledge. In addition managers could well assist trainers in enabling staff to take the new knowledge and skills gained from a training programme and transfer it into their everyday work situations. Their role in interpreting policy and procedures is often a key to the way staff understand and adopt them, while their attitude to a training programme can determine its success or failure.

Training for Managers

While the bulk of training programmes at present appear to be for operational staff, there is a strong belief held by many equal opportunities specialists that providing direct training for managers is essential if they are to provide any form of effective response to equal opportunities. Yet where there are training programmes held for managers there are often difficulties in obtaining attendance or interest.

The content of training courses for managers needs to be looked at in the light of their particular needs and the different concepts and strategy implications arising for them from equal opportunities. Sometimes managers can be reluctant to attend a training programme, as it may affect their position and authority were they inadvertently to expose their uncertainty or ignorance to others. Some of this anxiety is recognized by trainers but not always taken into account. Sometimes, too, trainers can feel quite intimidated by a management presence in their training sessions; likewise so can some participants feel daunted and inhibited at the prospect of revealing their thoughts about equality issues in front of their line managers or supervisors.

Where a training programme has real and total management support, and where the trainers have involved the management, the results that can be achieved are often considerable. It does not, of course, ensure total success, but those firms where there is some degree of genuine commitment from the top of the organization seem to be where some of the most comprehensive and effective programmes are taking place and the most profound organizational changes in the field of equality occurring as a result.

Key points

- How involved are managers in the training?
- Have any special programmes been set up just for management teams?
- What have you done to attract management support?
- Are there any special meetings where all the senior managers get together? If so, is that a possible communication channel?
- If you do train management groups, what is your attitude to them? How do you respond to them in a training programme and how do they respond to you?

Training for the Trainers

Trainers too need training and in most cases trainers are well aware of their own weaknesses but are not always in a position to overcome them. Even if they have the finances to overcome their weaknesses and obtain training there is often very little help available in local areas. Equality networks have grown in the past decade and some of this support and help could come from the existing trainers in a network or from elsewhere in an organization's structure. More attention needs to be paid to this area and some further work is needed to define more clearly the needs of trainers and examine ways to ensure that they do get the skill base they need and that their developing needs are also met. In addition to training needs, many feel the need for input and learning about organizational contexts, negotiation and influencing skills, consultancy skills and so on in order to further their roles beyond a reactive course-provision model.

Equal opportunities provision is far more than imparting knowledge to people. It engages participants in coming to terms with deeply held anxieties, fears and prejudices. Because of the developing spectrum of equal opportunities activities many of those involved in some capacity or other in the area find themselves drawn into a training role that they may not be fully equipped to handle. Yet they will try to do so because of their personal commitment and the pressures from others to meet their training needs. They should have adequate support and encouragement of the right kind to enable them to go some way towards meeting the high expectations of others.

New Standards and Qualifications for Trainers

Revolutionary new approaches to set a framework for occupational standards and vocational qualifications throughout industry and commerce is now taking shape in a bid to improve the quality of the British workforce. The task of setting the standards has been assigned to lead bodies, which have been formed with employers, the Industrial Training Organizations (ITOs) and non-statutory training organizations. The work to set standards is taking place now across sectors employing over 75 per cent of the working population including the following occupational areas:

* engineering
* construction
* retail and financial services

as well as in cross-sectoral occupations, for example:

* management
* training

- administration
- information technology

The initiative to set standards started some seven years ago with the recognition that a new framework for vocational qualifications and related training programmes was vital if Britain's products and services were to meet the world's highest standards. To this end, in 1986 the government produced a white paper entitled *Working Together: Education and Training*, which gave the Training Agency the task of producing a system of occupational standards across all industrial sectors by 1991. At the same time, the National Council for Vocational Qualifications (NCVQ) was formed to establish a new framework of vocational qualifications to be based on occupational standards. For the first time all qualifications would link to a common framework of five levels:

Level 1   Competence in the performance of work activities which are in the main routine and predictable, or provide a broad foundation, primarily as a basis for progression.

Level 2   Competence in a broader and more demanding range of work activities involving greater individual responsibility and autonomy than at level 1.

Level 3   Competence in skill areas that involve performance of a broad range of work activities, including many that are complex and non-routine. In some areas, supervisory competence may be a requirement at this level.

Level 4   Competence in the performance of complex, technical, specialized and professional work activities, including those involving design, planning and problem solving, with a significant degree of personal accountability. In many areas competence in supervision or management will be a requirement at this level.

Level 5   Competence in all professional areas above that of level 4. It includes the ability to apply a significant range of fundamental principles and techniques, which enable an individual to assume personal responsibility in design, analysis and diagnosis, planning and problem solving. Extensive knowledge and understanding are required to underpin confidence at this level.

The importance of these standards is that they represent a new way of describing people's abilities at work and will enable organizations to identify and match their training needs much more effectively. With the support of the Training Agency, the lead bodies are examining in detail exactly what is required for effective performance. It has been essential to establish the interpretation of the word 'competence' on which these new standards are based, and this has been agreed between the NCVQ and all lead bodies as follows:

> The ability to perform the activities within an occupation. Competence is the wide concept which embodies the ability to transfer skills and knowledge to new situations within an occupational area. It is competence in the organization and planning of work, innovation and coping with non-routine activities. It includes those qualities of personal effectiveness that are required in the workplace to deal with co-workers, managers and customers.

In Britain it is anticipated that this approach will bring the following benefits:

The nation There will be a common language of definition between work and education, embodied in a national qualification system which will provide a framework for improvements in the quality of the workforce and the competitiveness of British industry.

Employers Employers will have an accurate and relevant description of employee capabilities, and there will be a common language for organization description, workrole description, training and development objectives.

Individuals For individuals, there will be a common language of employee capability, which will be recognized across industrial sectors and which, through a new system of qualifications, can be improved and extended throughout life.

Occupational standards have three components:

- an element;
- a performance criteria;
- a range indicator.

The *element* depicts what people are expected to be able to do. This is expressed not in terms of activity, but as outcomes of one or more activities comprising a distinct role or industrial/business function. The *performance criteria* are the specific quality parameters by which successful performance in the elements may be measured and assessed. The *range indicator* defines the scope of the elements, that is, their range of applications.

The Training and Development Lead Body (TDLB) has had a challenging task to develop relevant standards for all the functions in training and development, which range from instruction to the more esoteric level where training and development form part of an overall organizational business strategy.

In developing the TDLB standards framework the analysis centred on the familiar training cycle:

- identification of training needs;
- design of training;
- delivery of training;
- evaluation.

In practice, different standards are combined together to form *units of competence*. They may be used to construct workroles or form building blocks in a framework for national vocational qualifications. The NCVQ framework is designed to allow an individual to enter at any level without having to attain the previous one.

The TDLB is aware of the crucial role it has to play in ensuring that the status of training and development is elevated and that the human resource element becomes an automatic part of an organization's business plan. Organizations are frequently being told to change their attitude towards training in that training should be regarded as an investment not a cost factor. The standards will provide a benchmark against which the effectiveness of a training budget can be measured.

For trainers themselves, the training and development standards will mean that they can gain public recognition for their achievements. A clear route will be set for career progression enabling individuals to prepare for promotion rather than the traditional path which is promotion first, training later. For employers the standards will also help with the inaccurate science of recruitment as individual competences can be accurately matched to job requirements. For industries and organizations facing constant change in technology the standards will provide an ever increasing bank of highly qualified trainers whether full or part time to carry out this task. The TDLB is in a unique position to bring tangible benefits to both employers and individuals alike. Britain will have a better skilled and more motivated workforce – an essential resource if Britain is to maintain her competitiveness in the world market.

The Role of Trainers

The range of general and vocational qualifications and competences required today must include a special ability to face up to and manage change. Whether a trainer's role is in initial or in continuing training, he or she is very much aware of the new flexibility in training systems. In job profiles too, the ability to adapt and change is, now and in the future, just as important as knowledge, expertise and attitude. In discussing the trainer's specific job skills, a number of questions must be answered:

*   To whom are we referring when we talk about trainers?
*   What are the new demands imposed by the roles they are now being called upon to perform, in the light of different training objectives and training structures?
*   What factors lie at the source of the obstacles to the development of such skills?
*   How are the suppliers of training for the trainers (the schools, employers and private and public training centres) meeting the demand (from public and private sector organizations, employers, trade unions, employers' federations, and the trainers themselves)?

In trying to understand the developments in a trainer's role and profile, the first step is to determine what differentiates the concept of 'pedagogy' in the field of vocational training, particularly the training of adults, from the pedagogical practices traditionally associated with education. Are the philosophy, strategies, methods and resources fundamentally different? If so, where do the differences lie?

A second question that must be answered for an understanding of the evolution in trainers' roles and profiles concerns developments in vocational training itself and the attitudes to be observed among employers, individuals and the public sector. The following points must be taken into account:

*   the specific training objectives (depending on new needs);
*   the changing content of training;
*   the organization of training;
*   training methods and resources.

The question of trainers' qualifications also needs to be analysed and related to the way the labour market operates for this vocational group. Is professionalization the simple answer? There is by no means a general consensus on the point and the debate is far from closed. There are different points of view, reflecting different lines of reasoning. The economy, for example, needs quality training, but has to contend with the constraints of cost and productivity. Trainers themselves naturally associate qualifications with their career development (internal and external mobility).

The debate on the professionalism of trainers is all the more important today since changes in approach, especially among employers, often generates new training strategies that are rarely stated in formal terms, and are certainly not institutionalized, with companies making use of their own internal staff to provide training. If this is in fact the trend, the relative importance of supervisory personnel seems to be growing. Their job profiles and training qualifications are certainly not of the same nature and scope as those of training professionals – and yet this supervisory function also calls for training skills. In the provision of training, what type of answers should be found to this set of complex questions, particularly as regards the continuing training of trainers (which appears to be emerging as the main route whereby trainers acquire their skills)?

A trainer is above all a subject specialist who is asked to 'transmit' his or her knowledge to others. It is usually at this point that he or she feels the need to acquire training skills through recourse to continuing training. But it should be borne in mind that there is a risk, in certain circumstances, of the trainer losing his or her own specialization, which also requires constant updating within the context of continuing training.

The provision of training for trainers is very diversified, ranging, for example, from very short, one-off courses to medium- or long-term courses, often fairly remote from the working world. A consistent, integrated pattern of further training in 'training' and 'subject' skills is not always possible for all trainers. The variety of approaches to the training of trainers has different effects on the quality of training and the labour market for trainers. And trainers are often faced with the problem that their employment is of a temporary nature.

Now that Europe is facing the challenges of upgrading the skills of its human resources and the quality of training, the question of the training of trainers is a focal point in debates on strategies for the development of human resources and in national and Community initiatives. Several programmes launched by the Commission of the

European Communities bear witness to this, as do national and transnational cooperative initiatives being set up throughout Europe.

The place of the trainer in a context of lifelong learning is essential but not always evident. With the introduction of new means and methods relying on self-activation and self-discipline many issues are raised, for example:

- The role of the trainer is questioned. The traditional relationship between trainer and trainee is changing with the use of these new training means and methods.
- The trainer who traditionally was the person who arranged the content and the pace of training now has a more supporting role.
- The trainee who traditionally was undergoing training now takes responsibility for his/her own training, his/her role gains new emphasis in the process of training.

Learning is often taken for granted when training takes place. However, learning takes place within the learner and training is not a synonym for learning. Telling somebody something does not guarantee that the message will be received and understood. If a trainer does not create a learning climate, the efforts made are likely to be abortive.

In a context where change and innovation are keywords, trainers are sometimes referred to as 'change agents'. Organizational changes can give rise to a diversity of training needs. Instead of simply reacting to situations which appear to have training implications, trainers will adopt proactive roles, consciously setting out to seek opportunities for change and exploiting them by whatever means are appropriate.

The acceptance of training as a valid means of contributing to the achievement of strategic objectives has influenced the functioning of the trainer. If training is central within an organizational context, trainers can play a major role in influencing structures and strategies. Corporate objectives are achieved by people doing their jobs. In order to do this, they need continuous learning opportunities. Another task of the in-company trainer is to make latent training needs manifest. This implies that they have to be able to identify and relate management, supervisory and employee training needs to business problems and opportunities.

The trend towards more trainee-centred training approaches and models also influences the trainer. This trend fits well within the evolution towards the stimulation of self-development, where responsibility for decision making concerning what should be learned, and how it should be learned, remains with the trainee. An example of such an approach is 'action-learning', whereby the essence is 'to be able to do'. The emphasis is not on the content of a problem; but on the process used or questions asked to overcome a problem. 'Trial and error' is another example of a trainee-centred approach, whereby the learner is experimenting. The learner tries out solutions to problems and observes whether or not they work. Such trainee-centred approaches do not imply that the trainer is absent during the whole training process; in fact he or she has a number of important roles to play including:

- guiding the trainee;
- providing information;
- facilitating learning and self-development by highlighting situations or examples or indicating to trainees where or how such knowledge can be obtained.

To use trainee-centred approaches, the trainer should be able to coach people in their process of problem identification and analysis, which is different from traditional training/learning approaches.

In the new training approaches, the training process is considered as a process of negotiation, whereby the trainer's role is to be a combination of:

- facilitator;
- mediator;
- counsellor;
- programme organizer.

The trainer is no longer seen as an expert armed with authoritative answers and solutions to problems, but as an equal member of a group, a resource on which the individual or the group can draw when necessary.

Trainee-centred approaches are of a participative kind, which imply a two-way communication stream. Empirical studies show that these are more conducive to lasting learning. If a comparison is made between the learner objectives and the role of the trainer, it can be said that if the learning objectives go beyond 'knowing that' (that is, the competences to be acquired are based on knowledge), the role of the trainer is no longer to be only an 'instructor'; he/she will also be a facilitator, a guide or a broker.

Learning objective	Competencies to be acquired	Role of the trainer
knowing that	knowledge	teacher/instructor
knowing how	problem solving	facilitator
knowing where	investigative	guide
knowing what/why	analytical	broker

The internationalization process will also influence the role of the trainer. Multinational target groups require specific approaches to the organization and the implementation of training programmes, especially if parts of a training programme are executed in different countries.

While it is not possible to make single succinct statements about what the role of the training specialist should or ought to be, it is necessary for them to have some personal and organizational concept of what their role should be. This is critical in determining their effectiveness and is influenced by a number of factors including:

- their career paths;
- values;
- background;
- ambitions;
- skills, expertise and knowledge.

Different trainers regard their role differently, variations include:

- trainers who see themselves as responding to organizational needs only;
- trainers who wish to play a part in developments and changes;
- trainers who like to act as a resource and centre of expertise for managers to draw on.

Added to such factors is the differing view of styles of training, which vary from a didactic instructional mode similar to traditional educational processes, to experts in the subject conveying expertise and knowledge to others on an experiential, almost groupwork basis.

It is important that equal opportunities specialists look at developing the trainer's role in more flexible, responsive ways. There may, however, be little incentive, apart from equal opportunities trainers' dissatisfaction with the present situation, to develop alternative and more responsive roles. After all, many will feel that they are already good at what they do, so why change it? There is truth in this, but we live in changing times. The future directions of trainers and the changing needs of organizations, as well as the future challenges of the equal opportunities field of specialism, oblige any committed and responsive trainer to consider experimenting and developing themselves and their field of expertise as well as each organization's perceptions of training. There is no single 'right' role but there is some need for flexibility, depending on what the trainer and the client want to achieve. Whatever roles trainers adopt they are bound to be affected by some of the following issues:

- expectations of others;
- own training experience and preferences;
- success of past activities;
- extent of management support;
- resources available;
- ability to influence others, amount of power they feel they have and their personal credibility.

Skills and Support

The skills, attitudes and knowledge required by equal opportunities trainers are similar to those needed by any trainer. While the range of skills needed by trainers is extensive, the areas listed below are the minimum requirements that anyone undertaking equal opportunities training needs to have to some degree:

- need to feel at ease with the range of issues surrounding equal opportunities;
- a broad knowledge of UK and EU equality laws;
- an awareness of own attitudes to 'difference';
- an expertise and knowledge of training design, methods and techniques, and in construction of materials appropriate to participants' needs;
- groupwork skills and an understanding of group dynamics;
- an ability to analyse problems and learning needs and difficulties;
- a knowledge and appreciation of learning styles;
- an ability to convey knowledge and ideas to others;
- an appreciation of the organizational context of training;
- a high level of presentation skills.

Equal opportunities trainers themselves tend to add to this list qualities such as resilience and a sense of humour. Many take a lot of battering in training sessions and have to listen to and challenge some amazing prejudice on the part of some of the participants.

Those undertaking equal opportunities work and training are concerned about their place in their organization and its relationship to their credibility and status. Access to decision making in an organization is often dependent more on a trainer's personal charisma and influence than on his or her status. The work an equal opportunities specialist undertakes is demanding, the job descriptions of complex proportions, the people doing the job are frequently alone and they can start to feel singularly unsupported once they become aware of the pay scales and role position. Those appointed to more senior ranks are effective not only in terms of remuneration but in status and often credibility as well. If there is some acceptance of the level of skills and expertise needed to do effective equal opportunities training work then it has to be recognized.

There is some evidence that staff working more than 60 per cent of their time on equal opportunities related matters are vulnerable to stress. The emotional overlaying and the intensity of the work becomes a problem. One way around this is to ensure that as far as possible some less stressful work is included in work schedules. The help and support of managers in restructuring timetables is inevitably important in achieving a more evenly balanced work schedule for trainers.

The Specification Facets of Training

Each facet may be defined in terms of the trainer's tasks:

Side 1   the training objectives

- co-define the functional capabilities (the practical expertise that is useful to and required by society) to be developed in the trainee(s);
- co-define the knowledge and the mental processes that the learner must acquire and master so that he or she can display those capabilities;
- co-decide on the content to be included (which means that the trainer must also be a subject expert).

Side 2   the context

- allow for the variety of target groups (young people, adults, novices, experts, etc.) and their projects;

- allow for resources (human, spatial and material) and constraints (number, timing, level of demands);
- make optimum use of in-house employees and their assignments (which means no longer being confined to professional trainers).

Side 3   learning strategies and activities

- allow for learning mechanisms, general processes of assimilation and the different ways in which those mechanisms are mastered by different people (personal cognitive styles or individual learning profiles);
- evaluate according to a pertinent theory, since the findings may be viewed very differently depending on the theory or theories adopted;
- devise (and apply) the most propitious intervention strategies and tactics (or methods).

Key points

- Has any training needs analysis been done for equal opportunities training?
- How does the organization tackle the needs of trainers in this area?
- If an organization has someone in a combination post (personnel and training, for example), what proportion of their time does the training take and how well equipped are they for it?
- What kind of training role do the trainers undertake?
- Is it possible to develop other aspects of the training role?
- Has adequate time been allowed for development and planning?
- Is adequate time allowed for monitoring, review and evaluation?
- If the organization uses external or freelance trainers, how appropriate is their style to the needs of the participants?
- What is being done to meet the various skill and support needs of staff doing equal opportunities work and training?
- Can some of the equal opportunities skills and expertise be used elsewhere in the organization to give them balance in their workload?
- At what level are they working in the organization; is it one that supports or undermines their role?
- Is their position and pay level comparable to other similar posts in the organization?

Training Towards Enhanced Competitiveness

Ensuring the long-term competitiveness of a firm increasingly depends on the qualifications and experience of its employees. Maximizing employee potential through providing full equality is nowadays recognized as a major contribution to company success. Investment in a firm's 'human capital' through effective equality programmes therefore forms part of any successful business strategy. Personnel planning and personnel development or, better, employee planning and employee development must be systematically linked to in-company training tasks.

Investment in training is generally only of benefit in the long term, and its effects cannot be accurately measured. Financial managers are therefore in constant danger of neglecting the need for investment in in-company equal opportunities training. The importance of long-term investment in training has implications for the 'image' and hierarchical position of initial and continuing training in a firm's organizational structure.

The successful implementation of future-oriented training concepts in a firm's internal structure is greatly facilitated if the training sphere is able to interact with the corresponding practical spheres on the basis of at least equal partnership. Provided that a firm's human resource management is a central division represented on the management board, the training sphere can be made part of corporate management as a comprehensive 'personnel development sphere'. Otherwise, training should be a separate management responsibility. This organizational structure emerges from the considerable importance that is even now recognizably attached to increasing investment in human capital. Similar organizational structures are emerging for small and medium-sized firms.

From this hierarchical position, in-company trainers can tackle their main task of ensuring that a firm has adequately trained employees in the right place at the right time. The bitter experience of recent decades with short-term training concepts geared to isolated areas of activity has made it clear that employees must be seen not as 'damage-prone cases in need of repair' but as living beings capable of development with individual features and extensive needs that should not be underestimated.

In-company training concepts, in-company future-oriented initial and continuing training scenarios geared to long-term economic gain, must be based on a comprehensive image of people, with a firm and a management identity developing on this philosophy. From this it follows, firstly, that the continuing training of employees cannot be promoted solely by, for example, isolated three-day seminars run by external trainers at hotels with sports facilities. Secondly, we need highly qualified in-company and external equal opportunities trainers who are familiar with the particular interests of a firm from many years of experience and have also undergone high-level further training in in-company and management training methods.

The in-company and management trainer must be an 'organization developer' if he or she is to be able to reconcile a firm's economic interests with working conditions that encourage motivation, creativity and equality. The in-company and management trainer is the 'presenter' of internal processes aimed at the further development of a management philosophy and corporate identity. Within this intellectual framework, people have an opportunity to further develop their individual potential, which is also to the advantage of the organization concerned.

Training in equal opportunities plays a number of important roles. It can be used:

- to help brief senior managers who are developing the equal opportunities policy and programme of activities;
- to convince key staff of the benefits of the policy and gain their interest and support;
- to deliver technical advice, knowledge, information and skills essential to the effective implementation of the policy.

Above all training helps make all employees alive to the importance of providing equal opportunities at all levels within an organization for everyone, to the benefit of both the organization and themselves.

What sort of training?

Training for equal opportunities includes:

- increasing awareness of the existence of discrimination and prejudice on the grounds of race, sex, disability, sexuality, age, and AIDS and HIV, both at an individual and corporate level;
- examining the nature of discrimination, both direct and indirect, and how it can occur;
- providing information and advice on the implications of relevant legislation;
- explaining to employees what is expected of them in terms of behaviour and assisting them to behave in non-racist and non-sexist ways;
- explaining the reasons for and importance of grievance and disciplinary procedures;
- examining the benefits to the organization of reflecting throughout its workforce the diverse society in which it belongs;

- identifying action needed to deal with discriminatory behaviour and processes;
- improving awareness of help that is available; e.g., EU assistance, local and national assistance, assistance for employees with disabilities, etc.

Benefits of training

For organizations, equal opportunities training will:

- improve the overall performance of an organization, by ensuring that decisions about employees are based on merit;
- help to ensure that individuals develop to the full and make their maximum contribution;
- enhance an organization's image and customer relations;
- ensure that all employers understand their responsibilities under the law as well as under an organization's equal opportunities policy.

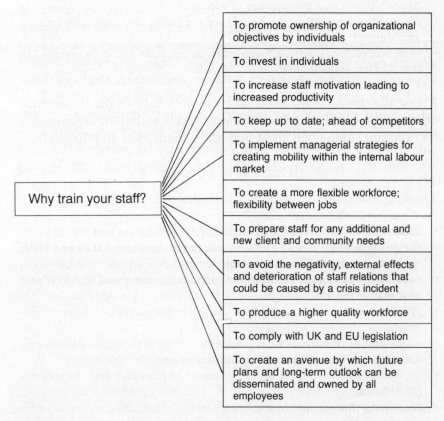

Figure 2.1 Persuading others of the need for equal opportunities training

Who should be trained?

All members of staff in an organization can benefit from training. Good equal opportunities training enables employees to increase their understanding of:

• the benefits which equal opportunities can bring;
• the reasons for and consequences of discrimination;
• their personal obligations under the law.

Managers at all levels and people involved in decision making in recruitment, selection, promotion and training are particularly likely to benefit.

How should the training be carried out?

Some organizations have incorporated modules on equal opportunities into existing company training programmes covering, for instance, induction, recruitment and management training. Others have established specialized training programmes such as group workshops on equal opportunities. Organizations that are not large enough to run their own training programmes might consider combining with another employer or buying training from a freelance equal opportunities trainer, a training consultancy or from their local TEC. Further information for smaller employers considering taking up one of these options may be obtained from the Institute of Training and Development (ITD) or one of the following organizations:

• Chambers of Commerce and Industry;
• European Information Centres (EICs);
• Training Access Points (TAPs) (these are computerized data bases that provide information on the range of courses available in a particular area, or training opportunities that are available nationally – TAPs are just one of the local information services that are provided through the TEC network);
• Industrial Training Organizations (ITOs);
• Colleges and universities;
• Open learning or distance learning centres.

The broad curriculum covered in equal opportunities training includes the following topics:

- the theory and practice of equal opportunity in the recruitment and selection process;
- the law and legal obligations, rights and responsibilities;
- the reasons for monitoring and evaluation, including equality targets and quotas;
- ways of helping people throughout an organization to set equality targets in their own areas of responsibility;
- the need to review the mechanics of the equal opportunities programme and its practical implications, including setting objectives.

Administration and Planning

Coping with the varied demands involved in running any form of training programme is part and parcel of a trainer's role. This includes the day-to-day logistics which will ensure that the courses run smoothly and that the trainer's life is as uncluttered as possible, so that he or she can concentrate on the training task and not on whether the tea will arrive on time.

The importance of this area is further highlighted by the fact that many of those undertaking equal opportunities training have to manage a series of multi-roles in their jobs, of which training is just one aspect, albeit a central one. Good planning and preparation is therefore crucial; lack of thorough planning and careful administration can obstruct even the most dynamic and potentially effective training programme. The following sorts of problems can interfere and ruin any potentially superb training activity:

- inadequate stationery supplies;
- poor lunch facilities;
- a lack of sanitary facilities;
- faulty mechanical equipment such as broken videos or overhead projectors.

While all of what can go wrong is not necessarily a trainer's fault, such foul-ups can so adversely affect the training process that a good trainer will do his or her utmost to check out arrangements well in advance, as well as to anticipate any potential difficulties. Course evaluation forms have often revealed praise for the trainer, while adding a caustic comment about the poor food, lack of beverages, uncomfortable seating, bad lighting, etc. And with the best will in the world these adverse comments cannot help but affect the overall participant response. The significance of the training environment is never to be taken lightly and the meaning these things take on for the participants can be powerful, often in quite destructive ways. Indeed some trainers might be forgiven for thinking that in today's image-conscious times, environment matters more to some participants than training programme content. In addition to the effect that lack of attention to detail can have on the actual training, it can also appear to trainers that the time and effort they have put into some of the administrative areas are disproportionate to the task.

One of the administrative tasks required to supplement training is the production of materials to support the case for training. It is rare for those responsible for training to be able to extract the information outsiders or each organization wants on each occasion a new demand arises. An accurate and detailed training record system has many benefits for trainers including:

- acting as a means of written persuasion on the reasons for future training requirements;
- acting as a means of reviewing current equal opportunities needs and future requirements;
- acting as a method for evaluating and monitoring an equal opportunities programme.

How it is set up will depend on the level of resourcing and trainer preferences, but it should take into consideration some of the following points and should enable the trainer to:

- identify at a glance all the training activities taking or having taken place;
- provide a comprehensive, up-to-date and easily accessible record of training activities;
- produce records on groups and participants showing who has been trained (for statistical and monitoring purposes to reduce any discrimination in training selection);
- adhere to data protection requirements if computerized;
- provide not detail for detail's sake but relevant and useful information;
- update records easily and regularly;
- observe confidentiality.

A trainer's guiding questions should be:

- What information do I need?
- Who else will need it?

- When will it be needed?
- How often will it be needed?
- In what form should it be recorded and reproduced?

Action Planning

Many trainers consider that the best way to meet training needs and avoid many potential pitfalls is to produce and adhere to an action plan. Setting such a plan enables both a trainer and his or her host organization to have a clear idea about what can be achieved and by when.

What is an action plan?

An action plan relates to measures identified in an organization's equal opportunities policy as well as in its training strategy. It enables all parties to it to get a feel of the actions to take. It allocates responsibilities so that people are aware of what is expected of them, and sets specific targets, aims and objectives. A good action plan sets deadlines for the completion of objectives and specifies how and by whom progress on each part of the plan will be measured and assessed. The shape it takes is determined by the size, sector and circumstances of each organization. Larger organizations may wish to consider developing plans for various parts of their organizations, which will feed into the overall action plan. Whatever the plan contains it is useful to map out a realistic timetable for completing the various actions and stages.

What should go in the plan?

Details of an action plan will depend on an organization's and trainer's precise aims and priorities. General details may wish to include or reflect:

- aims, objectives and priorities;
- monitoring methods and evaluation processes;
- timetables;
- equality targets;
- training implications;
- budget implications;
- personnel responsible;
- participants' views and expectations.

Benefits of an action plan

Establishing an action plan to take forward an organization's aims for the future is good business practice. A well-devised action plan helps to:

- focus everyone's attention on the main tasks to be tackled;
- encourage cooperation in achieving agreed quotas, equality targets and general aims and objectives;
- enable equal opportunities to be handled like any other management task;
- increase the percentage of people from ethnic minorities, women and those with disabilities in jobs or at levels where they are underrepresented.

Resources

The resources available to those undertaking equal opportunities training can vary from the plentiful to the meagre. Because equal opportunities trainers often lack any administrative assistance they sometimes find themselves having to do everything. Whatever the situation, a trainer has to handle the resources available to meet the training needs; if they are lacking then the trainer may have to explore alternative ways and means of supplementing the limited resourcing. Often getting the help of others is not too difficult if the training is sold effectively and the benefits to the various departments, individuals and the organization as a whole are outlined and reinforced on a regular basis. Such benefits can be got across to the workforce using a variety of means including:

- word of mouth;
- notice boards;
- staff bulletins;
- one-off 'newsflash' style bulletins;
- networking among the key equality personnel in an organization and disseminating the information in update reports through each department.

There are many possibilities for gaining access to resources of various kinds, some of which are outlined below:

- contacting local training institutions such as the local college to see if any placement students could assist in organizing a resource section;
- contacting some of the organizations listed in appendix 1; many of them supply certain material free of charge or for a very small fee;
- using an organization's own resources or local training scheme staff to design really professional-looking handouts on a desktop publishing system.

One of the best ways to handle planning, administration and a shortage of resources is to allocate specific time to it. Trainers can often be more inclined to spend time on the interesting and more obvious areas of work such as course design and training content than on other more 'boring' but equally important tasks such as administrative details. Trainers should:

- observe and think about the situation and identify resources available and the means to access them;
- adopt a creative approach, as often there are multiple ways of meeting trainers' needs;
- do the thinking in some detail, breaking it down as far as possible into manageable parts.

Checklists can be very helpful in planning events. They do not have to be compiled in one sitting but can be constructed as a trainer goes along, so that after one or two training events a trainer can put together a training checklist and order the activities in the way he or she likes.

Key points

- Have you considered other ways of resourcing your training?
- Have you developed an action plan?
- Do you keep records of the training?
- Do you record the group and section being trained?
- Can you produce information on demand about aspects of various training programmes?
- Have you explored the possibility of assistance from other departments or local sources?
- How much of your time does all the administration take up, is it diverting you from other tasks?
- Is much of the administration repetitive? If so, have you considered computerizing the basic administrative tasks, say in the form of a database, or developing a manual system to minimize repetitive tasks?
- Do you have checklists?

Organizing the Course Groups

Once the agreement for a training course has been reached, decisions need to be made concerning the selection and composition of course groups. It may be that the person doing the training has little or no input or control over this area, or perhaps it is not regarded as especially relevant. Yet many of the problems that trainers face in their work derive from the composition of the group and the dynamics that arise from that composition. People outside of the trainer's role often do not attach any importance to these issues – after all, if you are the trainer, you are supposed to be able to train anyone or any group. If possible, trainers need to try to influence this part of the training preparation, spending some time considering the best way to organize and manage those identified for training. There is no best way to arrange groups to fit all situations but there are two important issues a trainer may wish to consider in making a choice about the composition of their courses:

- different kinds of staff groups have varying needs in relation to equal opportunities training and these should always be taken into account;
- it is not possible, or even appropriate, to treat every course group exactly the same and teach the same content in precisely the same way.

The need for flexibility is important for trainers as well as participants. One of the many challenges of training is that no two sessions should be exactly the same, and the skill of the trainer lies not just in their expertise in the whole range of equal opportunities subjects but in their ability to put information over. The underlying basis always remains the objectives and key programme points; what can differ are the methods, exercises and style of delivery. For a trainer's own development it can be very useful to make sure that in each session he or she does at least one of the exercises differently from the way it was done in the previous session. It will help build up skills and meet the participants' needs in a flexible way. What works well with one group may not work at all with another. The trainer may feel convinced that it works: the problem is that a particular group may not share this conviction.

An important variable in any training group's response, and one that a trainer needs to take into account in deciding the composition of equal opportunities programmes, is the participants' experience of training. It can be easy for someone deeply involved in and convinced of the value of training to find it almost unbelievable that others do not share this view or that they may never have attended a training course before. Sadly, this is true of many participants arriving at equal opportunities training programmes. Undoubtedly, it often has a traumatic effect on training sessions and all who participate as trainer or learner. The issue for organizations is not that training does not exist – it does: the question is who has access to the training and who actually attends? Equal opportunities trainers are finding increasingly that many problems arise from the fact that a high proportion of their participants have no real experience of training prior to attending their courses.

The point has already been made concerning the complexity of equal opportunities training, the newness of some of the concepts and the crucial role of attitudes and prejudices in learning in this area. There is some debate about whether employees should be required or encouraged to attend equal opportunities training sessions. In the end this is undoubtedly a decision to be made by each organization itself, and the trainer or equal opportunities adviser needs to ensure that they advise the organization on this matter. Everyone involved needs to be clear about four issues:

- whether it is a policy decision;
- whether it is a managerial decision;
- why it has been taken;
- that it is not being undermined by different departments or sections.

Courses are often seen by participants as compulsory; they feel they have been ordered to attend and once there they may experience the process as one of indoctrination in a new orthodoxy.

One method of overcoming potential fears or dislikes of participants about training is to use some pre-course publicity to inform people about the course and prepare them for it. In large organizations it may not be possible to communicate personally with every future trainee, in which case just a handful of leaflets displayed on notice boards is better than nothing.

Group composition

If the needs of participants are different, the question which then arises is whether or not to mix the courses across different jobs, departments and levels inside and outside of an organization. A trainer also has to take into account three factors:

- the focus of the training programme generally;
- information available about the participants;
- the sorts of issues they are likely to raise.

Some of the key issues for consideration here revolve around the particular needs of different status employees, the effectiveness or otherwise of multidisciplinary training, mixed groups and needs and variable attendance and size of groups.

Mixed groups or otherwise?

There are several choices over group composition that trainers and organizations can negotiate. What needs to be watched is solutions and choices that owe more to the convenience of an organization than good training practice. It must be emphasized again that the composition of a group can and does affect the learning process. The real focus for the decision about group membership should be the purpose and objectives of the training event. It is when wider organizational forces and expediency operate that difficulties occur.

One of the key strengths put forward to support mixed groups is that they enable staff to see the work and perspectives of others and learn together, as well as to share anxieties and issues of common concern. While this is true, course organizers also need to remember that in many large organizations quite rigid role cultures prevail, in which people's power and status is informed by their job and position in the hierarchy. The trainer cannot expect the external environment to be left behind at the training door.

It is not only where the groups are mixed in job roles that difficulties can occur. When there are women in a group of men it may be quite difficult for the women: they may feel unable to assert themselves due to the sexism that can be shown, consciously and unconsciously, by the men. A woman's view can be taken less seriously and she may be given less space and opportunity than her male colleagues, both by the men in the group and by the trainer – perhaps more so if the trainer is a man. The same applies to the situation of black and ethnic minority staff. These difficulties can be replicated in any group situation where one or some of the participants belong to what is perceived as a minority grouping, whether determined by gender, race, sexuality, age, disability or any other factor. Such situations replicate the minority and discriminatory status and stigma, and trainers need to do all they can to minimize their effects.

Monitoring and evaluation can help but much is dependent on a trainer's awareness of the issues and the way in which the composition of a group is discussed, thought about and planned in advance. No one can ensure that these issues are removed completely but they can be anticipated.

Sometimes training has to take place in single work groups in preference to mixed or multidisciplinary groups because of the different situations of various staff groups. It is not easy for any trainer or training organization to arrange programmes for employees who work part time or hours outside of nine to five. The pay structures of some manual workers provide little incentive for taking up training. Many part-timers and some key staff groups (catering, administration, home care) are largely all women staff groups who are likely to have other commitments outside of work that restrict their ability to attend training courses. If trainers do not take account of such variables and constraints or they are unable to persuade an organization to modify conditions and meet the training needs of all staff, then some key staff groups could be left behind.

In the face of these difficulties some trainers are undertaking programmes in quite different circumstances from the usual training environments. One of the challenges of equal opportunities training is that of reaching all staff groups and then adapting the training model used to the place and the group at the time.

Size of groups and length of training

These two issues can be easily resolved or they can lie about constantly niggling at trainers and training organizers. They are two variables that will depend on the circumstances and the organization's view of the training. The size of training groups may be agreed in advance but can end up being quite different from what was planned. The size of groups in equal opportunities training sessions tends to vary from eight to ten staff up to over thirty. In negotiating training for large groups the following points should be considered:

- they can reduce the cost and the time and release problems, but they increase the likelihood of the training being ineffective;
- the larger the group, the more likely that people will not hear things properly or will be influenced by other people's behaviour;
- they do not always allow everyone to ask questions or to participate fully, however hard the trainer may try to involve the whole group by breaking it up into smaller groups and encouraging full feedback.

Arguing the case for smaller groups, which all research and experience tell us are far more appropriate and effective, may not be easy. Some of the problems lie in the way people in an organization regard equal opportunities training. They might concentrate on the information side only and reduce the importance of awareness raising and topical debate. It may well be that until trainers can persuade managers and policy makers to attend training sessions themselves, they will continue to put pressure on trainers to work with inappropriate numbers.

The same arguments arise in relation to the length of training programmes. Given all the issues, one day is an absolute minimum time for an adequate programme for any staff group. Two days will give a far better opportunity to explore and discuss issues and decide on courses of future action, equality targets and positive action measures. Decisions about length of training courses need to be taken in conjunction with decisions made about the content, size and composition of groups, and the training and learning needs of participants.

Key points

- How are your training groups arranged?
- Has there been any discussion or consultation on the best way to set them up?
- Have you experimented with different kinds of groups?
- How much say does the trainer have in deciding the composition of the groups?
- Have you experienced any problems in training courses that could be related to the composition of the group?
- How much past exposure to training have participants had?
- What steps do you take to ensure that staff arrive at training programmes prepared?
- Do you produce informative pre-course handouts or any other form of course publicity?
- Do people come to the course voluntarily or are they sent?
- What are you doing in the training courses to take account of the needs of minority groups in the session?
- What is the typical size of the groups you train? Do you have any control over this? If not, what arguments could you use to exert an influence?
- Where are you doing your training? Is there a need to take it out beyond the traditional setting in order to truly meet all staff groups' needs?

Checklist for organizing training

- consider room layout
- choose a venue that suits the size of the group
- make sure all of the group will be able to see and hear
- ensure lighting is adequate
- check any electrical equipment such as videos, televisions and micro-phones well in advance
- consider how guest speakers will be introduced
- wherever possible, time all speakers in rehearsal, taking question time into account
- check that visuals don't upstage the trainer's or trainees' view
- provide for coffee breaks
- check car parking arrangements if delivering a course at an unfamiliar venue
- write your speech in spoken English
- keep ahead of the group with notes/headings written on cards
- allow for the loss of trainees' attention
- emphasize and repeat the main points
- illustrate with examples
- be clear and brief
- avoid irritating mannerisms
- encourage trainee participation by dividing into subgroups to allow everyone to get involved in the training process
- with a small group, take questions as you go along but stay in control and don't lose your thread

3

Diagnosing Training Needs

An organization's willingness to apply a training solution to their problems can be rather like the doctor's prescription: 'All staff to take two days when needed.' If, as so often happens, the training solution is not fully successful, if the individuals continue to behave in ways the organization does not like or if they seem to continue to lack the skills required, then the training is seen as being at fault, despite the fact that some of the fault, if not most of it, may well lie in an inadequate or non-existent diagnosis of the needs which the trainer was trying to meet. If the issue and the needs are not properly diagnosed then the application of the 'right' solution may turn out to be wrong.

Many organizations tend to state training needs in broad terms which are intended to encompass everyone. For the organization it is often just an expression of intent. It is the job of the training provider, along with the managers and others, to translate that into a clear analysis of need related to the particular needs of each staff group.

In the field of equality of opportunity, many symptoms might reveal a need for staff training. Some of these are:

- there is a clear mismatch between the equal opportunities policy and practice;
- it is clear that staff are unaware of their duties to adhere to the policy or equality programmes;
- discriminatory acts are occurring, in which case training is needed to prevent a reoccurrence;
- equality targets have not been met, which indicates that positive action training might be appropriate;
- there is an imbalance between the numbers of men and women in particular sections or levels within an organization;

- an organization has failed to meet its quota to employ a number of registered disabled people;
- publicity or recruitment material fails to promote an equality ethos.

Training Needs Analysis/Audit

What is a TNA?

The development of new training opportunities has enabled many organizations to address training as a serious issue, not merely a side issue as in the past. In general terms, a TNA is a simple means of measuring the gap between skills available and skills required in a workforce, and making recommendations to bridge the gap. TNAs can either be undertaken in-house by a team of experts or an external consultancy can be brought in. Government funding for some forms of equality training such as the implementation of positive action initiatives may be available through the local TEC. In view of the importance of maximizing human potential through training, all companies should undertake a TNA at the point of recruitment planning or new product preparation. A training analysis must not be seen as an isolated event, since most aspects of business depend on the TNA achieving an accurate overview in the first place.

A TNA should gather as much information as possible about the following two questions:

- What skills and knowledge in the equal opportunities field does the workforce already have?
- What other skills and knowledge may they need to acquire in future in order to ensure the continued success of an equal opportunities programme?

The ability of an equal opportunities trainer to negotiate some space to carry out a detailed training needs analysis is clearly influenced by management willingness, as well as the allocation of time and re-sources. A TNA might follow the steps outlined in figure 3.1.

Key questions for training organizers

- Does your organization carry out a TNA in a thorough manner to establish the real gaps and needs in the provision of equality?
- Who generates the training needs for equal opportunities training in the organizations you work for?

- Do you respond to training needs as presented to you or do you attempt to diagnose the nature of the apparent training need before responding?
- Do you ensure that everyone affected is involved in assessing and deciding the needs?
- Do you ensure that everyone involved agrees the method of analysis?
- What do you do with the data collected?
- Do you share your conclusions with others?
- Do you use one method or a variety of methods to assess needs?
- If you feel that you haven't got the necessary time or skills to carry out a TNA, have you investigated who in the organization has?

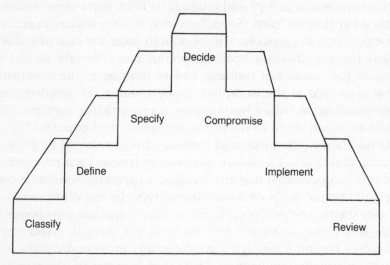

Figure 3.1 Steps to effective training needs analysis

Recent Changes in Education and Training

With only a few years to go until the year 2000, there is still too great a tendency to feel that the real major changes in education and training are yet to come. Many radical upheavals have, however, already taken place. It is just that some things evolve so slowly and gradually in education and training systems that their implications may not yet be apparent. This is especially true of equal opportunities training and education. The systems which have included both UK and EU laws and equality programmes have admittedly 'put the foot down on the pedal' over the past few years, but only in certain sectors. Among these upheavals (some of them revolutions) the following are examined below:

- the need for self-training;
- the restoring of learning to its central position;
- the primacy of the process and the project.

The need for self-training

The rate of growth in knowledge (doubling in less than twenty years) and the acceleration in advances in information and production technologies, as well as in human resource initiatives, mean that every professional has to devote a growing proportion of his or her time to learning, and lifelong learning. Never before has the fate of enterprises, social groups and individuals been more closely related to their capacity to learn. Soon, however, neither society in general nor employers in particular will be able to meet the cost of training if that training entails a break in production. Thought should be given to the manner of training, and to training in the workplace. What is needed in the workplace is self-training, as otherwise employers will be at risk of having more trainers than producers: 'We would be condemned to die of hunger, albeit well-educated.'

In addition to the manner of training, thought should be given to training objectives. The future is becoming less and less predictable, and it is inconceivable that any training programme should be confined to specific skills or narrow objectives. Each person needs to acquire internal resources on which to draw when the time comes to forge one's own solutions and to learn for oneself. Maximizing individual potential through a good equality programme is the best way to ensure this can happen. More than ever before, the trainer is the co-analyst of training needs. He or she is involved in:

- co-defining projects;
- co-setting objectives;
- co-planning equality targets and initiatives;
- co-observing schemes and equality programmes;
- and in the final analysis he or she becomes the co-partner in self-training.

The central position of learning

For centuries, individual tutoring (one teacher to one pupil) was considered the ideal, the privilege of princes. Since the early twentieth century, we have witnessed a growth in various attempts to individualize teaching (Parkhurst, Washburne, Dottrens, etc.) for the general mass of learners. Sixty years of the century had to elapse

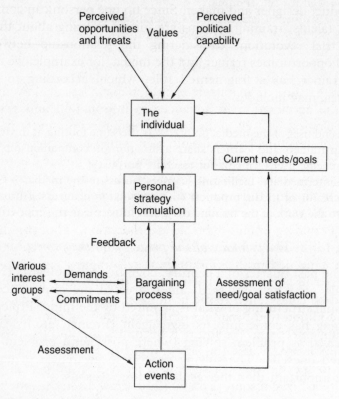

Figure 3.2 Interaction between training and the individual

before the work of Skinner and Piaget brought recognition of the central nature of learning in the training process.

Whereas in the past everything centred around teaching and the trainer (to take a simple example, think of the layout of desks in a traditional classroom), the trend then changed – to a Copernican revolution, with everything gravitating around learning and the trainee. Programmed teaching had lost the battle, but the individualization of learning was winning the war. Only temporarily, however, for recognition was also about to be given to socialization and the importance of the group.

Now at last the learner–trainer–environment triangle is changing. The trainer has become an organizer of an environment that promotes learning. The trainer's roles are proliferating and becoming more specialized. Formerly a purveyor of knowledge, he or she has diversified to become a counsellor, facilitator, confronter, as well as a product designer and maker. Since no one person can combine all these talents, training systems are forced to bring about their own industrial revolution. Considering the relationship between the equal opportunities trainer and the media, for example, we find that the trainer has a fragmented role, which, according to circumstances, may include:

- an end user of the media, on precisely the same footing as the learner, so that trainers and learners share a situation of 'companionship';
- a specific user of media for teaching purposes;
- an intermediary, facilitating learners' access to the media;
- a creator of media products (the production chain itself breaks down into the work of the training designer, subject expert, scriptwriter, etc.).

The primacy of the process and the project

For the past quarter of a century, cognitive psychologists (Norman, Novak, etc.) have stressed and restressed the importance of the personal structuring of what is acquired by the mind. Project-based teaching has come into its own again (Freinet, etc.): learning is perceived as problem solving (where possible, a problem one has defined oneself). The solving process in awareness of equality is more important than the result for three reasons:

- its influence on working methods;
- its effect on self-image, self-confidence and self-empowerment;
- the motivation it provides to solve other problems. (The integration of learning in personal strategies is just as applicable to adults as to children.)

Research on audiovisual processes, moreover, has led to the conclusion that the impact of a given process depends on many factors. The three main factors are:

- the objectives;
- content and resources;
- target group.

The only variable that always has a positive effect is that the onlooker becomes an active participant. One should be wary of a 'medium that does it all for the learner': what the medium does might have been an opportunity for activity of which the learner has been deprived. For example, a video might well occupy the learning space of a role-play exercise that might have provided more learning opportunity. Recent work by Kolb also points to the value of learning by doing.

These considerations affect training strategies in several ways:

- the tangible medium and format of information are of less importance than the relevance of that information to the learner's project;
- since the project is the result of variables, associated not only with the individual but also with transitional circumstances (constraints, resources), it is the learner who is best placed to judge whether the information is relevant to his or her project;
- it is crucial to the learner to be able to manipulate, (re)construct or (re)discover information.

Persuading and Negotiating: Making the Case for Training

This is one of the most common questions raised by equal opportunities trainers, yet it is extremely difficult to provide an answer that will work in all situations. In most cases a range of reasons will be more successful than just one, though the skill may lie in choosing the appropriate argument for the person or group being addressed. The problem is twofold: the employer, and the employees themselves. The prejudice and discriminatory attitudes held by some of those who can influence the provision of training seem hard to counter; they may be blatant and overt or hidden and subtle. A trainer has to transfer direct evidence into his or her negotiations with staff that equal opportunities training really does pay.

Too often in many organizations the signs that equal opportunities training is required are ignored until they all come together and suddenly the problem is seen as the responsibility of specialist staff, who are then placed under intense pressure to solve the problem for the organization. Training is seen as the immediate and easy solution. It is important to find ways to convey that it is more effective and time efficient, in terms of responses and use of resources both material and human, to anticipate the needs and tackle the problems before it becomes a disaster.

In general the difficulties for the potential training organizer and other equal opportunities staff lie in some or all of the following areas:

- In convincing the organization that training is necessary even when there are no incidents or groundswell of requests, no concerns, or a lack of data on the real situation or needs.
- In negotiating and persuading throughout all levels in an organization. To achieve this a trainer needs to look at concepts and perceptions of power, both formal and informal, in order to influence people in favour of training.
- In appreciating an organization's culture and in understanding where and how decisions are made. Anyone wishing to undertake equal opportunities work needs to be able to argue the case for training not only from within their own framework but from within a management and organizational framework too. This may involve learning new skills and acquiring new knowledge as well as becoming involved in other aspects of organizational life.

Influencing Training Providers: Key Issues

In influencing training providers, and monitoring and disseminating good practice, organizations themselves need to be made aware of the major issues relating to training for equal opportunities groups. To some extent, the specific issues will vary between different groups, and they will also vary from area to area, and companies will need to research the specific buyers which exist for the various groups in their own locality. In general terms, however, the key issues can be grouped into three main categories:

- access;
- contents;
- outcomes.

Access

Problems of access essentially fall into three main categories. Firstly, people may be unable to take up training because they are not eligible under funding criteria. For example, this is a problem for women when registered unemployment is used as a key criterion for eligibility for an organization's programmes.

Secondly, people may be discouraged from, or not apply for, training for a number of reasons relating to their personal circumstances or situation, for example:

- they may not be able to arrange affordable childcare;
- they may not have access to information about courses on offer;

- they may face financial problems relating to the benefits system;
- they may face language or literacy barriers in finding out about and participating in particular training provisions;
- the training offered may not lead to the type of work or promotion they want;
- they may feel that the training may be inappropriate or that they may not be able to cope.

In such cases providers need to ensure that personal circumstances are not a barrier to access. This can be done through policies such as effective marketing of courses and provision of childcare, open days and 'taster' courses, and financial or careers advice. It is clear, however, that organizations cannot generally rely on providers to identify and begin to remove such barriers. Effective research by an organization itself, including research on the barriers faced by potential trainees in its area, coupled with appropriate interest group consultation (community groups, representatives of the minority ethnic communities, disability groups), is clearly essential here; and it is clearly also desirable that each organization estimates the likely costs of different access-related interventions, and makes allowance for these in its contracts for providers.

A third category of access-related issues concerns not access for training *per se*, but the differential access/allocation of particular groups of people to particular kinds of courses. For example, certain groups may be underrepresented in certain occupational areas, or in the kinds of training opportunities which are most likely to result in employment. Although individual choice plays a role, it is clearly strongly conditioned by the assessment/advice/guidance offered. Here the role of the careers service, and other 'gate keepers' to and allocators of training is very important. Indeed, any points where advice on training or rationing of training takes place is a potential source of (often subtle) discrimination.

Contents

The contents and delivery of courses is clearly an area where equal opportunities should be addressed. Trainers need to be aware of equal opportunity issues in relation to course material, style of delivery, and the atmosphere or environment created. Course content may need to reflect the needs of a particular group and include confidence building/assertiveness training, and/or women only sessions. Similar examples do not apply only to women, but potentially to all the equal opportunities target groups, notably ethnic minorities (where a non-racist training environment is critical, where specific requirements such as language needs may need to be taken account of), and to people with various types of disability where aspects of the physical training environments, the duration of training and the materials used may need to take account of specific needs.

Outcomes

The crucial test of all training provision ultimately rests on outcomes. In order for organizations to take remedial action to deal with differential achievements by the different groups, two issues need to be tackled.

Non-completion Existing evidence suggests that the proportion of women, people from black and ethnic minority groups and people with disabilities completing training courses is lower than that for all male and all white trainees. This suggests that drop-out rates need to be monitored and the reasons for differences explored. These may well relate to content of courses and the training environment created within them.

Labour market access Outcomes may also vary among those who complete training in terms of their access to the labour market. Again the national evidence suggests, for example, lower proportions of people from black and ethnic minority groups and people with disabilities leaving training courses and finding jobs than is the case for all white people and all men and women. Again, the reasons for this need to be understood. Women leaving TEC schemes, for example, apparently do well in terms of access to jobs but in order to assess their experience of training properly, better information on the kind of job they secure is needed. To some extent, these problems may be alleviated by including development advice and guidance on job search within training programmes.

It is clear from these considerations that the role of employers is crucial in influencing the ultimate effectiveness of organizations' equal opportunities policies and practices.

Formulating Objectives

Good trainers do one thing very well: they help people to learn. This is achieved in two ways:

- by creating the conditions for encouraging learning;
- by recognizing and handling potential barriers.

The emphasis of any trainer must be on the needs of the course participants and on what the trainer can do to foster the participants' learning process. For many equal opportunities trainers the luxury of designing tailor-made courses with negotiated and detailed learning objectives is not a practical alternative. The assumption is often made that people's training needs are sufficiently similar to allow a standard set of equal opportunities courses with the same broad objectives to cater for everyone. It is also clear that the trainer has to handle participants with vastly different backgrounds, skills and knowledge, who are often there for quite different reasons. Therefore a central issue is whether their personal objectives can be reconciled with those that the trainer or the organization has already defined on their behalf.

Training and learning objectives

It is not possible or desirable to conduct a training programme without devising some objectives which ought to be drawn from a detailed TNA. Without such an analysis, objectives are often drawn from discussions with others concerned or involved in equal opportunities training, or set by the trainer on the basis of what they think the participants ought to know. *Training objectives are those broad aims set by a trainer from his or her point of view. They indicate the general intention and are vague about expected outcomes. Learning objectives, on the other hand, are very specific goals that tend to break down the broader training aims into outcomes, usually in the area of skills, knowledge and attitudes.*

Many existing courses are run on behalf of organizations and provide a course outline which includes the objectives. However, more often than not these are training objectives, not learning objectives. Learning objectives should be a set of objectives which enable the trainer to be explicit about what he or she is doing; they should be in addition to broad training objectives and be designed both to enable participants to measure their learning and to allow the trainer to measure his or her own performance. Objectives used are frequently closer to training objectives than to learning objectives, as they are not specific enough.

Learning objectives need to be divided according to the focus of the course into categories that examine:

- skills;
- knowledge;
- attitudes (cognitive, effective and affective areas).

Each area then needs to be linked into the evaluation techniques employed by the trainer to assess the effectiveness of the training.

Writing learning objectives

With practice, writing good learning objectives is not difficult. In drawing up learning objectives it is useful to follow these principles which can be found in one form or another in most training contexts:

1 What the learner should be able to do (their desired performance in skills/knowledge/attitudes/expertise) should be stated as precisely and unambiguously as possible. This means not writing a learning objective as 'To understand about equal opportunities and apply it to the work situation.' Rather break it down, for example, 'At the end of the course participants will be able to:

   - recognize prejudice and discrimination, both direct and indirect, as well as double and multiple discrimination;
   - explain the key benefits of equality in the workplace;
   - give examples of practices in their work situation where the new information can be applied.'

2 Use 'action' words such as: describe, evaluate, identify, produce, justify, state, list, prioritize, solve, formulate. Many descriptions of course objectives use verbs that are too general such as 'be aware of, appreciate, know, understand, realize'. The problem with these is to know how the trainer or the participants will know they 'understand, appreciate, realize' anything. Objectives should not be stated in a way that makes them ambiguous.

3 It can be difficult with the 'attitude' area to find precise words. As a considerable amount of equal opportunities training aims to address the question of attitudes and explore prejudices and values, it is imperative that the trainer not only knows what he or she is aiming to do but also has some way to measure success. Just doing it is not enough. This can be of particular importance where the training is intended to cover areas such as discrimination, race, sexuality and gender.

4 Objectives should be attainable. There is little point in having objectives that do not fit into the training programme or the duration of the course, or are so vague and ambiguous that they only serve to mislead. Neither should they be rigid and inflexible. Should the circumstances warrant, a trainer may well have to adapt the objectives or change them

completely to ensure the success of the training session. This is, however, rarely called for, and thorough planning should mean that most eventualities can be taken into account.

Key points

- Do you clearly understand the difference between training objectives and learning objectives?
- Do your objectives focus on learners' needs?
- If you have objectives, are they clear and unambiguous? and can they be linked to criteria to assess if they have been met?
- Do you let participants know the objectives so that they have a chance to say if they have been met?
- Are your objectives linked to training needs analysis?
- Are the objectives a clear part of the evaluation of the course?
- What observable behaviour will the objectives indicate?

4

Methods and Approaches to Training

Effective Training Programmes

Developing equal opportunities training responses that are effective and of good quality concerns everyone involved in the field of equal opportunities. Developing and implementing an effective training programme involves a number of key issues, for example:

1 *Negotiating and persuading people that there may be a need for training* Often the conviction that there may be a need for training is not shared by everyone in an organization, so that the person or department initiating the training programme may have to find ways of persuading others of the importance of their particular subject for training activities. In attempting to achieve this a trainer's arguments can be focused and rehearsed and important contacts made at all levels in an organization, which should be extremely helpful in later stages.

2 *Assessing the training needs of employees* Assessing the training needs of employees involves identifying needs, especially in relation to work practices, in order to establish what the individual does and the way that the subject of equal opportunities fits into their work.

3 *Formulating objectives – the purpose of training* Objectives are essential aspects of any training programme. They will be related to identified individual and organizational needs and are clear and precise goals to be attained as a direct result of a training programme.

4 *Making decisions about how to carry out the training, and about resources and strategies* A trainer's strategy involves the planning and philosophy of the training, and what he or she is going to attempt to do in order to achieve those objectives. It also includes how the trainer is going to set about the tasks they will have set themselves.

5 *Using practical and appropriate styles and methods for the training* The styles and methods used are related to the trainer and the training. They can include, for example:

- instructional;
- experiential;
- skills practice and development;
- groupwork.

6 *Decisions about training programme content* A trainer has to make detailed decisions about a whole range of key issues including:

- pre-course publicity and participant preparation;
- the use of language and terminology;
- the content and input;
- the use of handouts and audiovisual materials.

The eventual success of a training programme often depends on how well a trainer chooses in these areas.

7 *Selecting the right methods to evaluate the outcome of the training response* The outcomes are the changes that have resulted from the training. They are usually evaluated in relation to a participant's or group's job and the way they do that job. It is necessary to construct ways to measure and assess whether the objectives and aims have been met and the part the training programme played in that process.

Training Models

At present the bulk of the training effort in most organizations is being channelled into basic informational and awareness training in equal opportunities. It is clear that for the future additional kinds of training needs will have to be met, if only to keep abreast of continually changing EU legislation, and some organizations are already preparing for and trying out these new methods. These include:

- focused training for key groups of employees;
- specialist skills and knowledge attitude training for employees with direct involvement with clients with disabilities or with clients with HIV or AIDS or clients at risk;
- internal training for mixed groups;
- external training for local employers and local community members;
- employees who consider themselves or others as being at risk;
- specially identified service providers;
- staff who have an educational role with client groups.

Information and awareness models (IA)

This form of training is the most widespread at present and is being provided for staff at all levels within many large organizations. In these courses the focus is on understanding or learning about equal opportunities. The training content may vary in three ways:

• it may have only a loose connection with actual jobs;
• it may be quite specifically job orientated;
• it may have more in common with theories and ideas involving equal opportunities and its meaning in everyday working life.

The client/service aspect is almost irrelevant as the emphasis is on accurate information and education in its widest sense.

Disadvantages of information training

• tries to do a lot in a short time
• information input does not always combat anxieties
• has to meet wide diversity of individual needs
• raises issues related to much broader aspects of policy and management practices
• often driven by what participants want to know rather than what they need to know

Advantages of information training

• hard to exclude anything
• participants get accurate and up-to-date information
• people feel informed
• counters some bad aspects of misinformation
• chance to voice fears and anxieties
• impersonal element reduces fear and encourages debate

Content – what can or needs to be included in equal opportunities training programmes?

Learning objectives and training needs analysis can obviously help a trainer, but they are not always done and even when they are, they tend to become mixed up. Yet the nature of equal opportunities training, with its multiple issues as well as multiple angles of raising issues, means that the choice of information to be included needs to be selected even though it raises other questions, for example:

• Who selects the information?
• How do they select?
• What do they select?

As many training programmes are concerned predominantly with knowledge and only indirectly pick up on attitudes, a trainer needs to consider what parts of all the knowledge in the equal opportunities field are needed by the participants. Here the crucial difference should be between what they need to know and what they might want to know. In the end it comes back to analysis of needs and setting objectives, and the more thoroughly this is done the easier the informational choice will be.

Trainers and those responsible for training must look at the consequences of the attempts to cover so many issues and areas in the time allowed for basic information and awareness sessions. Overloading participants with information only serves to confuse, and leaves many feeling vague about what equality of opportunity is really about. Many organizations have come to realize that one-day information sessions are insufficient and have begun piloting two- and three-day courses. This has enabled trainers to focus more specifically on work-related issues which had been almost totally omitted before. If objectives are more specific and clear, content can be more focused. Many trainers prefer to go one step further and set contracts and agenda outlines with their host organization in advance of running a training session. Many of these include a breakdown of plans under these four headings:

- analysis of a firm's current situation;
- analysis of potential;
- setting of realistic targets;
- proposals for immediate and long-term action.

(Ideally, the last two activities ought to be timetabled.)

In conclusion, there is undoubtedly a real need for information and education on equal opportunities and perhaps one of the things to be done is for trainers to examine as many different ways as possible of presenting information or educating staff.

Attitudes and information

The nature of equal opportunities means that many courses deal with attitudes as well as information. Some trainers argue that people's attitudes can be changed with correct information, others believe that as long as behaviour is changed to more appropriate responses they are not concerned with the attitudes and prejudices harboured underneath. Whatever view a trainer takes, they must clarify where attitudinal changes are sought rather than simply making general statements about dealing better with issues such as sex, race, sexuality, age or disability by including references to them in a course.

Information and Learning

One thing that an effective trainer will do is to recognize that participants cannot take in a lot without time to reflect and absorb the information. This should follow from a thorough appreciation by a trainer of the importance of how people learn, and from adhering as far as possible to principles of learning in their courses. The learning cycle (see figure 4.1) is the standard tool of any trainer or training organizer. Sometimes it seems that training courses expect a direct line to (3) without (2). It is obviously difficult for trainers to reconcile participants' learning needs with the time they have for a course, participants' views and an organization's demands and requirements. However, for good training they need to stand firm on this. Not only is there a lot of information to be absorbed, but the language is new, it can go counter to commonly held views and prejudices, and stereotypes can get in the way. All the more reason for time to be allocated for reflection and understanding. Without reflection time, understanding will at best be mechanical and at worst non-existent. The departments and personnel responsible for the training must appreciate this and lower their expectations and

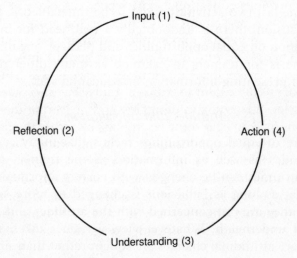

Figure 4.1 The learning cycle

pressures on the trainers and allow them greater flexibility to ensure that they can be successful.

Trainers need to be familiar with the ideas and concepts involved in learning and should seek to put them into practice in course design and facilitation. If this is done in a systematic way the information input is less likely to lead to information overload. Too often, if a trainer has some expertise in the area and detailed knowledge of a specific issue, participants can be on the receiving end of his or her own information overload. Trainers need to select and prioritize in order to choose what to say and to teach. For many participants much of the input is likely to be new, complex concepts presented using a new and difficult vocabulary. Many delegates may need:

* time to try out new ideas;
* time and opportunity to question and consolidate the input;
* time to reflect to ensure that they understand it for themselves.

Trainers, like participants, need to be reminded that when thinking about learning we tend to describe the 'tools' by which we learn, rather than the process of learning or the style by which we learn. Training courses can be greatly improved if these elements are taken into account by the trainer in designing courses. Participants will learn next to nothing if the activities and the approach do not use some of their preferred ways of learning which can be linked to the learning cycle. Also, the messages that participants bring to training from their previous educational experiences can often be reinforced if the emphasis is on content rather than on the process of learning. This is why many equal opportunities trainers prefer experiential methods. There is an erroneous view that because it is experiential and based on certain styles of learning, everyone will benefit. They will, but only to the extent to which a trainer has also taken account of other styles of learning in designing and delivering their courses. The sessions have to bear some resemblance to what the participants expect of training and education. It is important therefore that trainers make themselves familiar with the broad range of literature available on adult learning and learning generally. In addition, learning theory and research tell us quite clearly that the attention span of learners, no matter who they are, is limited. Making the training interesting and varying the activities does not on its own ensure learning.

Specialist Training

In view of the broader range of issues falling under the rubric of equal opportunities, this form of training is likely to be more in demand in future. It includes many specialist training courses such as:

- disability awareness;
- age discrimination in the workplace;
- AIDS and HIV infection and effects on the workplace;
- positive action training;
- EU training initiatives.

At present employers are not necessarily in active day-to-day contact with vast numbers of people clamouring for specific advice and training. This is, however, likely to change, and as it does staff working in the area will need skills and attitudes appropriate to the group's needs in order to enable them to be able to handle the issues raised. The training for these employees can consist of:

- a combination of top-up training adding to their existing knowledge and skills in the field of implementing equality measures;
- training to challenge discrimination on an individual level;
- training to develop additional skills and interest in equality;
- training to develop a detailed understanding of the issues of concern to new client groups.

Those employees whose role it is to teach or train those they work with also have specialist needs as they embark on talking to clients and trainees about concerns and issues so often neglected in the past.

Key points for human resource managers and trainers

- How would you categorize the kind of training you and others do?
- Do you have a choice in forms and level of training?
- How prepared are you to introduce new forms of training?
- Do you need to acquire new skills or knowledge to take on different forms of training?
- What information do you include in a training course?
- How do you select and prioritize?

- What part do others play in helping the selection process?
- Do your participants have the opportunity to reflect, challenge and really understand the issues and new information they are being confronted with?
- Do you mix attitudes and information? If so, how is it managed?
- Have you explored other ways of delivering information such as written handouts or course booklets which leave more time available for debate and understanding of attitudinal concerns?
- How far do you take account of learning styles, learning cycles and learning experiences in course design and implementation?

5
Working with Other Organizations

Much of the future work in equal opportunities lies in developing coordinated responses. These would bring together all those involved in equal opportunities work within local communities to effectively fulfil three needs of the community they serve:

* to plan;
* to train;
* to respond.

If such collaborative initiatives are to work, then training opportunities will need to be to the fore, as joint working will not come about by merely writing about it or willing it to happen. People from different disciplines and work cultures need to learn to work together for everyone's benefit. Their training needs to be done jointly. At present it is largely being done separately, though there is much talk of joint approaches to equal opportunities. Through campaigns such as Opportunity 2000, Act Up! and the Employers Agenda on Disability: Ten Points for Action Programme, to name just two, it is being encouraged at the highest government levels and many areas now have some kind of joint working group looking at the issues. However, there are not yet enough examples of practical shared activities, such as training, which should be high on any joint group's agenda.

Liaison groups or local or regional networks reflect a range of different responsibilities, aims and objectives. Individual organizations and local authorities do have their own strategies and plans, and yet in many regions a jointly developed strategic approach to equal opportunities and the training of staff is lacking. This might be partly due to an overdependence of one group on another, which as a result leaves little real progress achieved. Some training activities are set up by committed individuals, often working outside of these groups from which they are excluded because of the organizational hierarchies. There is considerable concern about the gap between the acceptance of the need for joint work and the lack of real collaboration. The situation is compounded by the fact that several recent surveys seem to indicate that there is no gap – almost everyone says they are doing training. Needless to say there is a vast difference between filling in a questionnaire and sending it away, and asking those concerned exactly what is happening. Much will depend on who fills in the forms.

Among the obstacles to collaborative training is the lack of higher-tier planning structures and systems in the main agendas and authorities. This makes it difficult to get multidisciplinary training on either management or political agendas.

Blocks to collaborative approaches

- Why work together?
- No single need; difficult to get the mixture or balance right.
- Cost and value for money; also problems associated with sharing the costs.
- Different organizational aims, priorities and strategies.
- No tradition of strategic planning.
- A lack of previous history of joint work; new territories always pose some new threats as well as opportunities.
- Lack knowledge about each other.
- Unsure of others' areas of expertise.
- Feel threatened.
- Key people unequal in status.
- Different language, norms, rules, customs.
- Geographical boundaries.

However, much evidence of existing duplication of effort and resources offers a real challenge and opportunity to share skills and knowledge to provide better services and more thorough training programmes.

Duplication of effort is one of the results of weak approaches to joint work and it can often be seen quite clearly in relation to training activities. Setting up training is time consuming and costly; yet there are many instances where different local organizations, even different departments in the same organization, are doing training for their own employees which directly replicates the efforts of others. Clearly this does little to promote consistency or collaboration in providing equal opportunities training and the services required to back it up. It also inhibits the trainer's own development and specialization. One of the strengths of different organizations lies in their own areas of expertise and knowledge around equal opportunities. This should be shared and developed in training activities rather than each organization doing all the training on everything for their staff or others. The current climate of competition and entrepreneurial enterprise is extending into training and it is likely to place more pressures on many of the training providers which could, if not tackled now, inhibit joint training initiatives in the future.

At present anyone, anywhere, can set up equal opportunities training courses. There are no requirements to coordinate or cooperate with each other and no imperatives on existing joint groups to include training in their brief. People are bound to be protective of themselves and their jobs, but in the long run it interferes with service delivery quality if different staff groups are getting different quality and quantities of training. Energy needs to be put into developing the following actions for organizations in the same region, same sectors or just among those that share a common interest:

- discussing joint philosophy and common approaches;
- developing consistency;
- sharing ideas.

Crossing Organizational Boundaries

The geographical sphere of influence can vary considerably and often seriously undermines joint approaches and activities. It is not uncommon to find individuals struggling to coordinate a number of organizational training activities in a whole range of different organizations, all within one geographical area. Many attempts can founder in the face of these problems. Yet it can seem a nonsense to insist on one's boundaries when equality of opportunity, prejudice and discrimination are no respecters of organizational limits. Ways have to be found around these issues and organizations themselves need to be more flexible if cooperative training programmes are to be successful. It is crucial to negotiate special arrangements to minimize the geographical limits that affect training planning. It may be for the larger organizations to take a lead in some way, if only to offer a joint venue to host courses. Without such influential groups lending their support to joint and shared training the trainer has to resort to personal or informal networking.

Involving the Voluntary Sector

The voluntary sector is, in some areas, playing a key role in all aspects of equal opportunities, including training provision. It is therefore crucial for the authorities to involve this sector in planning and organizing their responses. It is a truism that there is often considerable crossover of personnel from the voluntary to the statutory, with many people working in both as well as moving from employment in one to the other. The more this happens the better the networks and joint approaches appear to be, and even if there is duplication of training services and activities this can be less problematic as it is often the same people doing the same work. This is not a substitute for proper planning and strategic training approaches, but in the absence of these it at least bridges the gaps. In some cases the voluntary groups can use their expertise as well as their repudiation of boundaries to initiate collaborative action.

Developing Links with Local Community Groups, Organizations and Educational Establishments

Developing links within a local community can be a fruitful investment for any organization. Increasingly employers are recognizing the benefits of being involved in measures to improve employment opportunities for people in their local communities, particularly for certain groups. They acknowledge their responsibility to their local communities, which look to them for jobs and from which they draw their labour. They view their long-term interests as being linked to the education and skill levels of those communities.

What organizations can do

All organizations, no matter what their size or the nature of their business, can take a number of measures which will benefit themselves and enhance the economic development of their local communities. They include:

- networking with other employers, local authorities and Training and Enterprise Councils (TECs) and Local Enterprise Companies (LECs);
- giving support and assistance to local community groups;
- linking with local schools and colleges;
- taking part in conferences, seminars and local activities to promote equal employment and training opportunities;
- sponsoring or setting up training for non-employees to help equip them with the skills, experience and confidence that they need to compete for jobs on equal terms with others.

Benefits of community action

The main benefits are:

- employers stand to gain a broader-based supply of motivated, educated and trained people;
- an organization will be seen as one that wants to develop and maximize the skills of employees and potential recruits; in other words, as one that provides equality of opportunity to enable all members and future members of its workforce to reach their full potential and not be held back by the negative forces of prejudice and discrimination;
- the opportunity to make a useful contribution to the local community which will help secure future prosperity for both an organization and the community;
- helps to secure a good company image.

Community groups and organizations

A number of community groups and organizations are in an ideal position to assist organizations to develop links with the community and achieve a better understanding of the needs of local areas. These include

Training and Enterprise Councils and Local Enterprise Companies TECs and LECs are led by local business people, representatives drawn from the voluntary sector, trades unions and local authorities. They give employers a major voice in training, vocational education and enterprise support in the community. They have a responsibility to identify and meet the special training needs in their locality. They are well positioned to assist organizations in arranging local training and employment events.

Racial Equality Councils (RECs)   RECs have been set up in areas where substantial numbers of ethnic minority people live. They work in partnership with the Commission for Racial Equality and the local community. Their role is to advise and provide support for the local community. They are well positioned to advise employers on how to provide assistance to local ethnic minority groups.

Equality Exchange   The Equality Exchange is sponsored by the Equal Opportunities Commission. It is a network of employers, trainers and consultants who share information and experience on good practice in equality of opportunity in employment. The exchange of information is facilitated by conferences, seminars and networks on subjects of interest to employers. Membership is open to any organization that has an active interest in developing equal opportunities in employment.

Employers' Forum on Disability   The Employers Forum on Disability is a national employers' organization which is sponsored by a number of major employers. It aims to advise employers on developments relating to the employment and training of people with disabilities.

Placement, Assessment and Counselling Teams (PACTs)   PACTs are locally based disability advisory and placement groups based in jobcentres and employment offices. Their role is to advise employers, employees and potential employees on local services and assistance for the education, employment and training of people with disabilities.

Committees for the Employment of People with Disabilities (CEPDs)   These are local committees set up as advisory bodies under the Disabled Persons (Employment) Act 1944. They consist of people with local knowledge, interest and expertise on disability employment issues. They can offer advice and assistance to employers and the local community on issues relating to the employment of people with disabilities.

Other action

This might include, for example:

* Setting up links with local community groups, churches, mosques and temples.

- Setting up local networks for people interested in equality matters to meet and exchange information on good practice and arrange mutual training and other activities.
- Developing an equal opportunities resource centre between a number of organizations or interested groups in a local area.
- Setting up joint positive action programmes in response to local community needs; enlist the support of the local TEC to assess what needs are the greatest.
- Working with the local careers service.
- Offering school and college students work experience, work shadowing and visits.

Employer groups

Individuals can help to start or become a member of a network of local employers. This will help in a number of ways, including:

- acting as a pool of expertise and experience;
- serving as an exchange of ideas and good practice;
- helping to identify and solve problems of mutual concern.

There are already a number of groups in operation. For individuals or organizations interested in setting up or joining such a group the local Racial Equality Council, the Employment Department's Race Relations Employment Advisory Service, the Equality Exchange or the Employers' Forum on Disability is able to advise.

Liaison and Collaboration within an Organization

Liaison and collaboration is not something to be evoked only in relation to external agencies. It also needs raising internally in all organizations. The structure of many large organizations does not make it easy for collaborative work and in some places equal opportunities training activities seem to bring out the worst inter-departmental rivalry and attitudes. Examples of this often arise where an organization has no one person responsible for equal opportunities work. Even without a designated coordinator it is poor practice (especially with a major initiative like equal opportunities training and activities) not to inform each other of departmental activities.

Even if there are agreements that each department will do its own training, there must be some shared agreements about:

- aims and objectives;
- learning outcomes;
- training content;
- duration of courses;
- philosophy and focus of training;
- evaluation methods.

If organizations have or are considering setting up working groups on equal opportunities, these groups must address themselves to training strategies and approaches and promote integration and cooperation, not concentrate on narrow sectional interests. Where organizations have appointed a working group to examine equal opportunities, integration is less of a problem, as it is simpler for a highly visible unit to make an impact on the system than for one individual to do so.

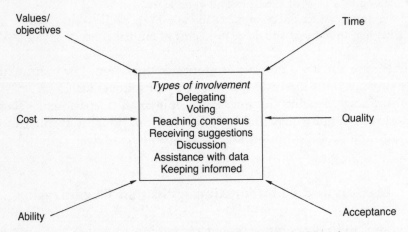

Figure 5.1   Factors influencing methods and styles of involvement

Key points

- Are you working alone or with others?
- Do you have or do you belong to any joint working groups?
- What are the obstacles to joint working?
- Who do you have to persuade about the benefits of joint working?
- Who attends the local joint planning group? Do they have training on the agenda?
- Is there a gap between the written and spoken rhetoric and the practices in your area?

- Have you discovered duplication in the organization or departments you work in? What has been done about it? Why is it happening?
- How much duplication are you guilty of?
- What are the strengths of your training programme? How does that complement the strengths of other programmes in the area?
- Is the voluntary sector included in your training?
- Does the voluntary sector provide training in your region?
- What is your relationship with local community groups?

Part II
Training Programme Content

6
Problems and Possibilities

Handling the (Sometimes) Negativeness or Unpopularity of the Subject

Equal opportunities face the individual and the organization with a subject that is surrounded by negative extremes. It is not easy to avoid them nor to find a way to minimize them. It can, however, be easy to learn from them by handling negativeness and prejudices not by objectifying the person who holds them but by broadening the issue to include everyone. In fact, the greater the number of prejudiced comments and discriminatory suggestions made, the better the chance of issues being raised of their own accord and not being imposed on participants. This way, issues are likely to be regarded as more relevant and more connected to the subject as a whole than those that are forced at participants through even the most well planned of exercises. So it is essential that it is the issues themselves that are confronted and not, however tempting it may be, the person who raises them. Evidence shows that to antagonize individuals spoils the training atmosphere and usually results in a group concluding the day more racist or sexist and less responsive to equality of opportunity than they were at the beginning. This of course runs counter to the aim of equal opportunities training, which is to give participants the opportunity to explore their own prejudice and discrimination, to understand how it evolved and what processes ensure that it continues, unless some fundamental changes take place.

Even when employers declare that everyone must receive some training to help put the equal opportunities policy into practice, they are inadvertently falling into the negative. The notion that everyone needs to be trained reinforces the peculiar views and attitudes already widespread. Both the person who feels familiar with the theories and practicalities of equal opportunities and the person who considers it completely irrelevant to their job might feel angry that management considers they need training. Equally, management might later wonder why they have failed to gain the commitment of their workforce and forget that voluntarism rather than enforcement is the essential prerequisite to commitment. Trainers have to face the difficulty of dealing with a subject on which there is often little in the way of positive information directly relevant to the people whom they may have to train. A common concern among those in charge of planning training is how to avoid a training course or informal workshop becoming a series of do's and don'ts. This is an area that a trainer has to be careful about; he or she must be aware all the time of what they are projecting in the way of information and attitudes. They must also strive to keep up to date since even a list of do's and don'ts changes over time, with the introduction of new legislation or new information on AIDS and HIV, for example. It does appear that the more information a trainer attempts to tackle, the greater the potential problems. Therefore it is crucial to keep a tight rein on course objectives and content and make activities relevant.

A trainer can do much towards reducing the negativeness of the subject, for example:

• Make the point, at least once, that equal opportunities benefit all members of an organization, not just those people that fall into a minority group. Give examples. Don't wait for an argument to start or boredom to set in before this point is raised and discussed.
• Respond to each negative question, answer or opinion with a positive one.
• People rationalize their views in peculiar and powerful ways, and pre-thinking and planning could circumvent some of the inherent difficulties trainers face in explaining equal opportunities issues.
• Give easy or single explanations that can explain people's negativeness in a way that encompasses, and not isolates, people's own views.

Participants' Views

Equal opportunities training sessions involve the trainer in dealing with a cross-section of the public and some of the common-sense views held by people in general. Trainers have to handle them in such a way as not to invalidate them as individuals but ensure that they question and reformulate some of their invalid assumptions. Particular attention needs to be paid to legitimizing those fears and anxieties held by some participants in their own 'rational' framework, created by the information they have and the prejudices they hold. A trainer's role is to train, not to impose their own personal appraisal of legislation, government campaigns or any of the other wider initiatives in the field of equal opportunities that lie outside of their control. In explaining equal opportunities, trainers need to recognize that not everyone has grasped the theories about prejudice and discrimination, let alone the finer points about causation and cure. For any trainer, time taken away from the pressures of running courses to analyse and understand participants' views pays off handsomely in the end.

Key points trainers should consider include:

• Could you do any pre-course survey to assess the range of views participants bring to the course?
• (If you cannot do this) how else could you be prepared for the various views?
• Is your training input able to deal with heavily entrenched 'common-sense' views presented as if rational?
• How do you counter the kind of views that participants bring to the course?
• Have you found out enough about the potential learners' jobs?

The single most common obstruction in the process of equal opportunities training is the fear among participants of exposure. People are very often afraid to say anything at all for a number of reasons including:

• fear of being ridiculed,
• fear of offending a fellow participant, or being offended,
• fear of being probed too deeply by an over-zealous trainer,
• fear of being singled out as an example.

To avoid silence and to encourage a healthy platform for debate a trainer should consider:

• At the beginning of a course, together with the usual practical details about lunch breaks, smoking rules and health and safety considerations, say a few words about the nature of the subject, the contents of the day's programme, its potential sensitivity, and about the aim of the day not being about sitting in judgement and comparing each other's stance on the subject, but about learning from the issues raised. Emphasize that in order to do this, respect and tolerance of each other's cultural and ethnic backgrounds, as well as personal characteristics and opinions should be shown throughout the day.

• Gain the consent of participants by reaching democratic agreements on certain ground rules. Questions that could be discussed are: can spokespersons for subgroups be alternated so as to reflect everyone's views? what are the issues of concern? can we risk exposing our guilt/innocence about certain topics or would the process be too risky? Experience shows that gaining consent not only acts as an icebreaker, but also increases group confidence which in turn enables debate to flourish.

• Some trainers send out pre-course questionnaires, and the participants bring these with them to the course. An alternative to this, which would enable the trainer to pick up some of the ways of thinking about equal opportunities that the participants will bring with them, is to have questionnaires returned prior to the course so that the trainer has enough time to analyse the answers and adjust the depth of explanations to take account of participants' views. Also, this undoubtedly helps trainers to devise exercises and activities to counter common prejudices more effectively.

Confidentiality

Increasingly, the issue of confidentiality comes up in, among others, HIV training sessions, and discussion tends to revolve around the 'right to know versus the need to know'. Many trainers have discovered that the official policies on this area may well be undermined by different rules that operate for different groups. The maintenance of confidentiality about an individual's circumstances is an accepted principle in professional groups and applies to people with AIDS and HIV infection as much as to anyone else. However, the issue also affects staff groups not used to confidentiality issues and lapses can occur with some shattering effects on the individuals, whether clients or colleagues. Each organization needs to provide trainers with clear guidance about confidentiality and trainers who deal with sensitive information regularly need to address the issue of why confidentiality is important in their training courses, especially when the participants are unused to the ethos of confidentiality. It is an issue where the trainer needs to consult with managers and others in order to be clear about what rules operate in each section so that they can separate out custom and practice from any actual policy.

Amount of Material to be Covered

A common concern among trainers is the amount of material to be covered. For two reasons this fear is not likely to go away:

- In the last decade the range of equal opportunities issues has broadened and their impact has increased through the introduction of new legislation and the inclusion of new topics such as ageism, AIDS/HIV and sexual orientation.
- In a recession, the training budget is often the first to be cut, so that greater course content has to be fitted into shorter timescales. Even in an economic peak the demands on staff mean that few can be released from their normal duties for more than a couple of days. With the increased demands on staff time, and the trend towards reducing the average length of training courses, maximizing course content and minimizing training costs, the volume of material to be covered often causes both trainers and participants to lose sight of their original goals.

Other factors, including

- the pressure to train,
- the desire to give participants their money's worth by filling their heads with facts,
- inadequate training needs analysis,
- little management involvement,

often mean that trainers have to cope with comments and needs that really should be dealt with in separate staff training sessions. Trainers often find, for example, that they spend a large part of the day discussing that particular organization's policies and procedures. It might be that there is a lot of hostility towards these caused in the main by senior managers imposing them on staff without bothering to explain them. This tends to raise many separate issues that divert attention away from the main points. Also, a training course might be one of the few occasions other than Christmas parties when staff get together, so rather than be treated as a serious event, there is a tendency to regard a training course as a purely social event or an escape from the routine of everyday life.

As all good trainers know, by connecting issues and enabling participants to make their own connections, by encouraging enquiry and facilitating methods of putting training course objectives to purposeful use, problems associated with the volume of material to be covered need not be insurmountable. The ability to connect a day's events, discussions and 'sections' along a single thread towards a meaningful whole is the mark of a good facilitator. The natural order in the acquisition of knowledge is from the vague to the precise, from the rough outline sketch to the detailed picture, and from the provisional and inaccurate approximation to the refined and balanced truth. This, of course, illuminates the rule formulated by psychologists that we should learn things by the 'whole' method rather than by dividing what is learnt into obstructive sections. So, by adhering to the whole subject and not hidebounding our training by rigid compartmentalization, a large part of the problem of the amount of material to be covered can be addressed. Other aspects of the problem can be handled or solved by:

- An initial meeting, face to face, or followed up in writing if by telephone, to discuss and agree training goals. This involves agreeing upon the training content and, just as important, agreeing upon what will not be covered. At this stage it is useful to discuss and agree upon any way in which the participants might plan for the day, and decide upon anything they should bring to the session. Once the goals have been discussed and set, the ability to achieve them is often more a question of the trainer's ability to introduce, debate, close and connect issues, more than participant diversion.
- Setting a clear agenda at the beginning of a training course.
- Presenting facts, such as legal points or medical information, as hand-outs, which need not intrude upon the awareness raising of central issues. A good handout, well presented and thoughtfully written, can serve a multitude of purposes.
- Requesting, not demanding or expecting, cooperation from participants, and explaining about time restrictions and the volume of material to be covered.

The Focus of Training

In some cases there are difficulties relating to the actual focus of the training. Much seems to depend on the person who is doing the training and their particular bias and interest as well as what they feel comfortable in handling. Sometimes the focus of the trainer and the organization are not fully compatible, or it may not be easy to discern any underlying thread which leads to a particular focus for training sessions. As a result a trainer may be struggling with several possibilities and trying to control the boundaries between the different emphases. Possible focuses are:

Accurate information   The focus is on key facts and concepts.
Job issues   The focus is on the job that people do and what they need to know.
Issues only   The focus does not deal much with information and facts; participants already have many facts and a lot of information. Focus is on issues that arise out of, for example, anti-discrimination laws.
Combating discrimination   Equal opportunities is an area complicated by issues of discrimination and prejudice and unless the trainer deals with these issues nothing else can be achieved.
Attitude awareness   Until the participants have explored their attitudes to issues such as sexism, racism, ageism, etc. little progress can be made in giving information, combating prejudice or developing skills.
Best service delivery   There should be no discrimination or difference in service delivery. Training focus is what the participants need to know about the group of people they are going to work with.

None of the different focuses need be mutually exclusive, although some trainers may feel strongly enough to place their entire emphasis on one focus to the exclusion of the others. Whatever the focus, ideally it should be the result of a joint decision by management and trainers, and if possible the views of the participants should be considered too. Too often in the past, trainers have made the decision on their own, based on personal conviction, without necessarily communicating it clearly to the organization or the participants.

The advantages of joint decision making about the focus of training include:

* trainers can plan training and prepare content more precisely;
* participants are more aware of what is in store and what is expected of them;
* potential complaints about training not meeting needs, or straying off the point will be avoided.

Trainer Bias

Bias and influence in particular directions have a strong and inevitable presence in the work of all trainers. As much as they may wish to be neutral and to present an objective case throughout, the very nature of training means that is not possible. The methods they choose, the content they decide to highlight, that which they accidentally or deliberately play down or avoid completely, the way they handle questions and participants, all exhibit the trainer's views and style, and some would not hesitate to call it bias, or to put it another way, prejudice. To this must be added the fact that many of those involved in equal opportunities training are people with a high personal commitment to the issues. They cannot really be otherwise and employers often recruit them for that very reason. Such concern has often sprung out of a high degree of personal exposure or experience of one particular issue, which in time has been joined by concern over all the other issues that fall under the rubric of equal opportunities. A woman, for example, might have been introduced to the subject through a combination of the failure of men to treat her seriously as a colleague, with daily doses of sexual harassment thrown in to further undermine her professional status. Although she may understandably be biased towards sexism and sexual harassment as issues, she nevertheless has a duty to embrace all of the issues (for which she is being paid) and avoid boring participants with excerpts from her personal case history.

Many trainers have been recruited from a background of high involvement in the voluntary sector where many of the issues of equal opportunities were first raised. Here they have developed considerable expertise, experience and often strong views which they have brought to their work with employers. The advantages of this need to be balanced with a concern to avoid the possible pitfalls. Some of these are:

• a tendency to train over the heads of participants;
• a tendency to assume a certain level of knowledge already exists, without first checking that it does;
• a confrontational approach towards participants who voice an opinion which runs counter to the trainer's strongly held views.

To avoid these pitfalls arising in the first place, or to correct them once they have been highlighted, it is useful to check the feedback and evaluation that arrives from participants. If a significant number of participants comment in their feedback that a trainer was biased, the trainer can safely assume that he or she was indeed biased and strive to become less so. Also, setting and agreeing the agenda between trainer and participants at the beginning of a training course can help to avoid any tendency to stray off the point onto pet topics.

In some circumstances the most suitable trainer an organization can employ is one who not only suits their group most closely, but one who knows the subject most closely. A trainer with a disability, for example, can often put their everyday expert knowledge to better use for participants than a non-disabled trainer equipped only with his or her textbook expertise can. This kind of 'natural' bias is often particularly appropriate for specific equal opportunities issue training courses. For example:

• a trainer with a disability for disability rights or disability awareness training;
• an HIV positive trainer for courses about the confusion that exists over concepts such as high risk group/high risk activity and infection/contagion.

Attitude Change and Social Consequence

Though it may not always be apparent, equal opportunities have touched most aspects of society, and work practices have felt the impact as much if not more than other areas. Not only has this made people look at their social and work behaviour, it has also exposed attitudes and vulnerability in people. Nowhere is this more apparent than in training sessions, and in HIV/AIDS training in particular. Fuelled by tabloid newspapers and its association in this country with such major taboo subjects as drugs, death and sex, it arouses profound fears and reactions that are completely disproportionate to the reality of people's situations. Although it is only contagious in specific limited circumstances, it is seen and responded to as if it were highly contagious and as if verbal contact alone with an infected individual would condemn another individual to the debilitating symptoms of AIDS within minutes of contact. This issue comes up repeatedly in training sessions. Even when it is regarded as less of a mystery, it is still often seen in this way and is regarded as needing highly specialist knowledge and responses. Add to this the near-panic reactions, inflamed by tabloid journalists, expressed towards people and groups whose stigmatized behaviour is seen as closely associated with HIV infection, and you have some very difficult attitudes to handle in training sessions. In all of the issues associated with equal opportunities, often it seems that knowledge is not enough to counteract the fears and myths, prejudices and stereo-types, but in HIV training sessions the course content can even reinforce these fears by putting a heavy emphasis on prevention, risk activities, health and safety, survival figures, life expectancy and death rates.

It is often in a context of resistance to inevitable attitude changes, with its contradictions and dilemmas, that equal opportunities trainers are expected to operate. One day they can feel positive and optimistic about their work, and the next very negative and ineffec-, tive. Often, this is because people resist change and will do all in their power to prevent it from taking hold. Trainers are vulnerable since they represent the bearer of news about the changing role of women in society, AIDS statistics, unemployment among ethnic minorities, for instance, and in so doing might appear as if they are in control of such facts, and leave themselves open to blame. No matter how obvious it may seem, one of the most effective ways of avoiding this is to make it very clear at the beginning of the day that you are merely a catalyst delivering facts and debating issues with the participants.

Terminology and Language

The growth of organizational equal opportunity policies has been met by a growth in the number of organizations requesting training and a growth in the range of individuals receiving training. Because of the range of people being trained many trainers have found that they have had to pay careful attention to terminology and language. In order to do this, these points should be considered:

• The handouts and materials in use should be examined for clarity and appropriateness in the light of the group being trained. This does not mean being patronizing or too simplistic but making sure that the information is presented as clearly and concisely as possible, and in addition encouraging or prompting participants to ask questions about information contained in handout material. Some of the material in use falls short of this criterion: for instance, 'It only takes one woman to fill a book with personal examples of sexual harassment' is meaningless unless accompanied by some examples, or 'Despite intensive scientific

research epidemiological studies indicate only three modes of transmission of the virus that causes AIDS' means little to many people.
* The preparation of information is rarely geared to each participant
  group because this would be too time-consuming, but with a little
  forethought coupled with a good word processing package just one
  handout can be modified dozens of times in accordance with each
  group's needs in mind.

A trainer comes to a course with a thorough familiarity with the
language and concepts, while the average participant does not. If the
concepts and issues are to be properly addressed then some degree
of familiarity with the terminology is required. Clear and consistent
definitions are needed, but on the other hand a trainer who constantly corrects participants can be a real irritant. Also, the language
we use to describe specific behaviour varies between individuals, and
what does not offend one may offend another. The trainer needs to
find out how to make such descriptions without offending or opening up feelings that will only serve to hamper learning. The words,
comparisons and analogies that a trainer can use with a group of men
who have volunteered to explore the roots of their sexism in a male
awareness training course can be quite different from those used
with a group of men upon whom such training has been imposed by
management. This is not to say that there is an element of con-
descension present, just that there should be an awareness of, and
sensitivity to, the groups present on the course. Ultimately, it is a
matter of trainers anticipating each coming session and deciding on
the ways to handle it which fit the needs of the group.

Confronting and Handling Conceptual Confusion

There is sometimes confusion about ideas needed to appreciate and
understand some of the issues related to equal opportunities. The
trainer needs to handle this sensitively, and take particular care in
the way he or she approaches the issues. The style used in training
should attempt not to be prescriptive in any way as the trainer is
constantly having to clarify any uncertainties. A prescriptive approach will contradict this and make the job harder.

It is important not to confront participants with how wrong they
may be in their understanding as, particularly at the start, any
revision in views ought to come from them. They need to make the

adjustment as the session continues. It has to be personalized as a process of discovery for each individual, not the trainer telling them how it is and how they need to think and behave. This area is difficult, and trainers need to look closely at it, as sometimes they may think they are not being so directive but in fact the way information is being handled and conveyed is having this effect.

Clearly, because of the range of people involved in equal opportunities training as well as the range of participants, there can be no standard 'question and answer' list of confusing issues. However, those that crop up most often include:

- the meaning of prejudice and discrimination, their differences and similarities;
- confusion over equality meaning the same treatment for everyone rather than equal treatment based on individual needs;
- the difference between positive action, positive discrimination and affirmative action;
- the notorious 'equal pay for work of equal value' provision of the Equal Pay Act;
- the different interpretations that can be put on statistics;
- the difference between high-risk group and high-risk behaviour in connection with HIV transmission;
- the difference between infection and contagion in connection with HIV transmission.

Many of these problems can be avoided by:

- The use of very clear and concise definitions.
- A short discussion at the beginning of a course about what equality of opportunity means; despite its familiar ring in most organizations, few people are completely clear about what it means and what it entails.
- Statistics should be used very carefully, if at all. They are most useful if presented in a way designed to make the course think about the way they are used, the problems in using them and what they really tell us.

Suspicion

Trainers have to deal with a lot of information, much of it new to the course participants, and one area of concern lies in participants' bias, interpretation and suspicion of the explanations offered by the so-called experts involved in equal opportunities. As people's attitudes and understanding vary, what they hear can be crucial. For the trainer it is important to consider how to deal with these questions and what school of thought is promoted.

Another problem which arouses suspicion is the lack of definitive answers to many questions which arise out of equal opportunities issues. The often absurd questions and examples that participants can come up with should be seen not just as their being difficult, as some trainers might be tempted to believe, but as coming from their genuine fears and anxieties. It may be useful for a trainer to react not by confronting these questions but by addressing the underlying fears and feelings. This may be difficult, depending on the time available and the skills of the trainer, but those who have tried it report it as being very helpful, and it can move a course from a negative place to a very positive one. This is where group dynamics skills and interpersonal skills are extremely valuable. Skills can be supplemented by paying some attention to the psychology and understanding of prejudice. In addition to this, trainers should pay attention to the literature of learning, as it is important to realize that much of what they tell the group will be lost fairly soon after the course and that at least 20 per cent of participants will not believe what is said because of their set of beliefs and attitudes. These will block the receipt of information so that some employees will remain untouched by training. This is something the trainer needs to ensure that the employer already understands, and it is a wider issue for an employer who wants employees who will carry out the organization's policy, practice, views and culture. Trainers should also try to appreciate that in general the majority of participants will not share even a fraction of their interest and enthusiasm for the subject, and if these feelings are to be generated, it is up to the trainer to generate them.

The Use of the Expert

This is one area where there is considerable disagreement on the part of different trainers as to whether or not to use people in their training who will be seen as experts, for example, a medical expert to give the facts about HIV transmission or a gerontology expert to hold forth about ageism or demography. Disagreement centres on whether or not an expert narrows or widens the credibility gap. Often, the language and information given is inappropriate and confusing. It can also of course undermine the trainer's role, as what the expert says is likely to be regarded as more important than anything the trainer contributes.

The use of people with HIV infection or AIDS is a contentious issue. Of course, some of those who are already involved in equal opportunities training are people with HIV infection or AIDS, and were in the job before the disease was discovered. Also, in much the same way as patients with various disabilities are used in medical training as part of a learning programme, some people with AIDS or HIV infection are used in equal opportunities training to put across various issues and points to the participants. Whether this is appropriate or not is up to the trainer and his or her host organization to decide, and experience shows that the following points should be considered:

- Who is to be used and what should they say? Some speakers from external agencies can present themselves and their ideas in ways that could be confusing and be taken wrongly by course participants. Some assistance in presentation skills might be needed: after all, they are not the trainer.
- What will be the effect on the person? The questioning and intrusion of participants as well as their often outspoken views can not only be counterproductive to a learning process, but potentially extremely hurtful to the guest expert.
- The way a person is introduced has to be very carefully thought out: a clumsy or dramatic introduction might be regarded as sensationalism or tokenism.
- It could reinforce existing stereotypes and prejudices.
- Introducing a very healthy-looking individual who happens to be either HIV positive or a registered disabled person can have a very definite impact on participants' faith in the course.

Whatever the trainer decides, the credibility and personality of the speaker is frequently an important factor in the success or otherwise of the enterprise.

Explanations of Policy

It is unfortunately true that for many organizations the written word of policy is often separated from the dilemmas and contradictions of practice. In many training sessions, participants can come up with many examples of contradictions between policy and practice, and the fact that policy is drawn up separately from practice yet is supposed to inform practice is often a source of irritation for many participants. Of course, reference has to be made to an organization's policies, but concentrating too much on policy matters tends to give a training course a feeling of paperwork divorced from real work, which in turn encourages previously lively participants to switch off.

In an ideal situation, the trainer should either be able to explain policy to staff so that it is integral to the training, or alternatively should be able to devote a session exclusively to policy. Equal opportunities courses related specifically to policy implementation can bring out a 'policy versus practice' discussion as part of an introduction by requiring that all participants read their equal opportunities policy in advance and come armed to the course with a list of questions about its relationship to practice.

Many of the problems over policy can be handled by taking the following steps:

- Ascertain (at an initial meeting) how familiar staff are with the equal opportunities policy, and how much say they had in its formation and its implementation. Have they all been given a copy and has specific time been set aside to read, understand and query it? Are they aware of their individual responsibilities to comply with it and put it into practice?
- Read the organization's policy, anticipate questions or problems that participants might have about it.
- Look for specific links between the policy content and course content and use them as examples.
- If possible, use the organization's own policy to highlight issues and clarify points; this is much more relevant to participants than another organization's policy or a sample form designed by experts.
- Introduce a policy as just one of the interfaces between theory and practice; while not undermining its significance in any way, strive not to regard it as the only means of achieving equality in the workplace.

Range of Methods Used in Training

Method	*Objectives/advantages/points to watch*
Case studies	• to draw upon wider points
	• to relate to work issues

watch out for

- need to be well prepared
- purpose and focus to be clear
- relevant to group

Discussion in small groups
- ideas shared
- inter-group communication
- more can speak

watch out for

- clear focus and questions
- elect different spokespersons
- composition of groups
- feedback important
- ways to mix groups

Experimental exercises
- relates learning to each individual's needs
- starts from participants' standpoint

watch out for

- can be seen as silly
- purpose needs to be made very clear
- unease some people have about such activities
- needs high trainer skill levels

Expert input
- useful if trainer lacks expertise about a particular issue

watch out for

- make sure person is prepared and focused
- participants may only hear that piece of information
- could undermine trainer's role

Group processes dynamics
- can enhance learning
- helps group communication

watch out for

- difficult to control
- high trainer skills needed

Handouts
- to expand information
- to follow up the session
- for future reference

watch out for

- preparation and layout
- language and terminology
- linking into the course content
- presentation to the participants when and how?

Questionnaires
- assist learning
- may be used as pre-course work
- explores group's understanding
- training aid

watch out for

- may be seen as test preparation
- takes time to prepare
- should be course-specific
- does questionnaire's content match course content?

Role play
- applies the information and ideas
- makes discussions more relevant
- helps learning
- offers opportunity to practice skills

watch out for

- participants do not like these activities
- need preparing
- trainer skills high
- confused with acting, not seen as real
- just plain silly

Statistics
- to put issues in a broader perspective
- to inform

watch out for

- why are they used?
- can be used by individuals to dissociate self from issues
- how are they interpreted (is the glass half full or is it half empty?)
- who has compiled them and from what sources of information?

Videos
- breaks up sessions
- can provide additional information
- can put information into context

watch out for

- which one to use
- quality of discussion afterwards important
- participants nodding off

Evaluating Training

Acquiring skill in training in all of its forms, like acquiring any skill, depends upon the principle of 'feedback'. One of the most well-established and practically important findings of the scientific study of learning is that the subject must be kept informed of the results of his or her attempts to make the right response. This depends on the feedback of information regarding the success of the attempt. The same principle applies in training: the trainer learns by receiving back information as to the success or failure of getting a message across.

Evaluation is a crucial element of any training and learning process. Without it there is no certainty that a course has achieved any of its objectives. Without it there is no base for modifying and developing existing training activities or planning future training events. Evaluation is really a research exercise to estimate a programme's impact, followed up by implementing negotiated improvements.

Many trainers report that they have neither the time nor the resources to evaluate their courses and, even if they had, they still lack the expertise to do so properly. As a consequence, very little systematic and planned evaluation of equal opportunities training takes place.

Trainers should check the following ten evaluation key points:

- What level/kind of evaluation is best suited to your group's needs?
- Are you clear about the benefits of evaluation?
- Do you regularly review the content and materials that you use in training courses?
- Are you sure that the training produces benefits and results beyond immediate reaction responses?
- How do you check that participants have retained the information correctly?
- How do you know the courses have any long-term effect on participants' views?
- How do you measure the effectiveness of your activities, content, handling of sessions?

- Do you collect any information about the training in any planned or systematic way?
- On what basis do you judge success?
- What do you do with the evaluation sheets?

The assertion that an evaluation system is essential to establish the value of the training and should underpin any training activities is not made lightly. There cannot be a full training process undertaken without evaluation, as its omission leaves nothing but uncertainty. Evaluation is the systematic collection of information of various kinds needed to make training effective. It should reveal the extent to which objectives and training needs have been met, and what future training strategies are required to ensure that participants continue to develop their skills and knowledge. The benefits of evaluation are not confined only to obtaining immediate reactions from participants. They include:

- feedback on the quality of design and delivery of training and effectiveness of learning;
- information on how well it reflects the organization's needs and whether training is the appropriate way to meet those needs;
- help in demonstrating value for money; is it the best way to use resources?
- help in involving, influencing and persuading others and developing relationships with managers and other sections;
- establishing credibility;
- research to enable trainers to improve their skills.

What forms of evaluation are taking place? Many trainers carry out on-the-spot evaluations throughout a course, and in response make minor adjustments in input, materials and exercises. Also, there are plenty of follow-up reaction sheets around. Trainers like them because they give immediate feedback, usually of the positive kind. This, however, is more because of the nature of the reaction sheet than any particular brilliance on the part of the trainer, since in general they tend to measure enjoyment rather than learning. Very positive evaluation may indicate that the participants have enjoyed the course, or that they have been entertained, or that they just liked the trainer; it may not mean that the course aims have been met. Less glowing accounts may indicate that the participants felt challenged on personal issues, that they may have had to grapple with their own prejudice, and that ultimately the course aims were more closely met.

The more effective kinds of reaction sheet being used are those that link the responses into the context of the objectives of the training session. Another kind of evaluation is undertaken through the use of action plans, which can relate the learning back into the workplace. Some trainers require the participants to pair up and contract to monitor each other's action plans at agreed intervals; this method can be a useful personal support mechanism. Both of these methods link objectives to learning outcomes.

Course: Equal Opportunities–Basic Awareness Training

Notes:

- leave 20 minutes at the end of the day to complete the evaluation sheet
- 'introduce' the sheet: explain that it is not a test
- if participants prefer, they may leave their sheet anonymous

Learning objectives:
At the end of the course participants will be able to:

- distinguish between prejudice and discrimination, their causes and effects;
- have a basic knowledge of words and phrases associated with equal opportunities;
- have a basic knowledge of anti-discrimination legislation and handouts for future reference;
- state and assist in implementing methods of monitoring and evaluation in the workplace;
- identify examples of sexism, racism and ageism in their workplace and give examples of practices in their work situations where the new information can be applied;
- know what organizations might be useful in assisting with advice, information and handling a legal case.

Questions:

1 In a sentence explain the difference between prejudice and discrimination.
2 Name two methods of monitoring an equal opportunities policy in the workplace.
3 Name two methods of evaluating an equal opportunities policy.
4 What laws might a person who feels they have a justifiable sex discrimination claim use?
5 Name three organizations where you could go for help in putting together an equal pay claim.
6 What kind of follow-up training do you consider you need?

Figure 6.1 Sample evaluation questionnaire

Checklist of key points

- handling the negativeness of the subject
- participants' views
- confidentiality
- amount of material to be covered
- the focus of training

- trainer bias
- attitude change and social consequence
- terminology and language
- confronting and handling conceptual confusion
- suspicion
- the use of the expert
- explanations of policy
- range of methods used in training
- evaluation

7
Training Programmes

Methodology

The best methods to use for a course depends upon a number of factors, including:

- the number of people to be trained;
- the culture of the organization;
- the trainer's own preferences;
- resources available;
- the location of training.

It is possible, however, to conduct most equal opportunities training sessions using a wide variety of methods. No issue is best delivered using just one method or type of exercise. A combination of those listed below helps to stimulate a creative environment which encourages participants to learn.

1. Role play, to highlight basic issues associated with equal opportunities. For example, role-play exercises on job interviews or harassment in the workplace.
2. Small discussion groups on equal opportunities terminology such as prejudice, discrimination, victimization, with feedback to whole group using flipcharts to stimulate interchange of ideas.
3. Quizzes to generate discussion on specific equal opportunities issues, and to highlight the need for improvements in the provision of equality.
4. Videos and other visual aids.
5. Case studies.
6. Question and answer panel sessions using issue experts. For example, someone from Opportunity 2000, a disability rights expert, a successful woman returner, etc.

7 Seminar and lecture style training delivery using overhead projectors is an appropriate learning method for covering many issues such as equal opportunities legislation and policy formation.

8 Manuals (ring-bound for ease of use) are an ideal training resource for trainers running a series of equality courses with the same group, since they act as a continuing source of reference during training, between courses and afterwards.

9 Checklists of equality do's and don'ts.

10 Brainstorming in small groups to stimulate as wide an appreciation of what equality means in practice as possible.

Awareness Training

Who should attend?

- first-time and middle managers as an ingredient in early management training;
- specialists, experts and consultants in human resource issues;
- all new staff as part of their induction programme;
- all staff involved in training to enable them to get a grasp of their responsibilities and obligations in the field of equal opportunities.

By the end of the training programme delegates will have:

- understood the basic principles that underpin equal opportunities, including the main definitions, legislation and issues surrounding barriers and obstacles to the implementation of equality measures in the workplace;
- explored ways of introducing equality measures in the workplace;
- designed an action plan to incorporate and continually improve equality measures in the workplace.

A training programme should aim to cover the following information as a minimum:

- examine the major issues underpinning equality;
- the main UK legislation governing equal opportunities;
- main definitions such as prejudice, direct and indirect discrimination, racism, sexism, etc.;
- examine ways of developing policy and translating it into practice.

Racism awareness training (RAT)

Since mass immigration of minority ethnic groups first started in the early 1950s, official policy towards race has passed through three broad phases:

1   *'Colour blindness'*   Immigrants and their children were officially treated no differently from anyone else. However, the signs of racism such as slogans like 'no dogs or blacks', were ignored.
2   *Control of numbers*   In response to perceived tension in working-class areas, and the Notting Hill riots in the 1950s, the Commonwealth Immigrants Act was passed in 1962 in an attempt to control the number of immigrants.
3   *'Integration' and cultural pluralism*   In the late 1960s the then Labour government tackled problems of racial discrimination. Roy Jenkins, Home Secretary in the 1966–70 Wilson government proposed a strategy which offered 'equal opportunity, accompanied by cultural diversity, in an atmosphere of mutual tolerance'.

The 1968 Race Relations Act extended the scope of the Race Relations Act (1965). Previously only 'public places' were bound by the law; the 1968 Act extended legal protection to include employment and housing, and established a Race Relations Board to investigate discrimination.

However, further studies showed that subtle and widespread discrimination remained. The 1976 Race Relations Act reflected concern that racism was often powerfully expressed below the surface. It recognized that equal opportunities had to be promoted rather than allowed to emerge over time. The Commission for Racial Equality (CRE) was set up and given responsibility for taking the lead on this.

In the mid 1970s the atmosphere shifted from an assimilationist and integrationist stance, which assumed a coherent society, to one which channelled extra resources to minority ethnic groups. The eradication of racism had become a legitimate object of policy. The recognition incorporated four main points:

• that the different ethnic communities are indeed very different;
• that minority ethnic communities are oppressed;
• that minority cultures are as important to them as majority cultures are to the majority and should be understood by the white community;
• that part of the job of understanding different cultures is an appreciation of white racism rooted in the past.

These four strands formed the background to racism awareness training. RAT has two aims:

1   The aim of RAT for black people is to help them understand the historical factors which have led to racism and to develop a black consciousness to use as a basis for personal growth and development.

2 For white people, it aims to help them become aware of themselves as white people, and to recognize the history of their negative and often oppressive relationships with black people.

RAT is delivered in three distinct ways:

* by black trainers for black participants;
* to racially mixed groups;
* sometimes by black trainers for white participants.

It developed to explore the conflict between black and white people, and the terminology used in training reflects this. The use of all black and all white groups is to create a safe and secure environment in which participants can explore their feelings about racism.

Sexism awareness training (SAT)

Sexism awareness training, in the context of employment, is made up of a variety of different strands. These include:

1 assertiveness training;
2 empowerment and self-development;
3 networking;
4 the use of mentors and role models.

It covers the acquisition of both skills which enable women to be effective at work, and those which help them to develop a political awareness about how things are achieved within an organization.

1 Assertiveness training The essence of assertive behaviour is equality. Assertive communication is usually defined as that which embodies three characteristics:

* clarity;
* honesty;
* directness.

It is the ability to express one's needs, opinions, feelings and wishes in an appropriate manner without violating the rights of another person.

Being assertive is not being aggressive. It is understanding oneself and communicating successfully with others. It involves coping with attitudes from others, and also with some self-negating attitudes which may originate from within.

Techniques include:

- being able to make clear and concise requests;
- using body language as well as voice;
- saying 'no' to others' requests when it is difficult to do so;
- disagreeing without either humiliating the other person or stepping down yourself;
- expressing feelings and handling criticism.

2 Empowerment and self-development Individuals are encouraged to take personal responsibility for their own development. Self-development allows women to broaden their understanding of themselves and the effect they have on others. It allows them to move from the personal to organizational and managerial concepts.

3 Networking The need for a wide range of contacts is part of an ever increasing political awareness among women. An analogy with the 'old boys' network is often made. Many organizations are now actively encouraging and supporting women's networks. For example, commercial firms such as British Gas, colleges and universities, TECs and LECs.

4 Mentoring and role models Mentoring is the use of a top-management person as a role model. A problem can be finding enough female role models, but this problem assumes that role models are swallowed whole and therefore have to be women. In fact it is perfectly possible to use the best aspects of different individuals, and whether the models are men or women often becomes irrelevant.

Mixed versus women only groups Single-sex groups provide an environment in which women often seem more prepared to take risks, and it is only by taking risks that personal development occurs. Increasingly, development programmes are offered in different forms, for instance:

- women only;
- modular;
- mixed residential.

Organizations or potential trainees may choose the most appropriate methods. Some women, for example, might choose to learn management techniques through distance learning such as that offered by the Open University, to develop personal awareness by joining a network and to increase their skills by attending short modular programmes. It is important, however, that women's management training is kept close to and involved with mainstream management development.

Male awareness training

Although less established than racism awareness training, male awareness training (MAT) follows similar patterns in practice and in implementation. Male awareness training has three aims:

- to give males the opportunity to explore their own sexism;
- to provide a platform to debate and understand how this evolved;
- to debate and explore what processes ensure that it continues, unless some fundamental changes take place.

Evidence suggests that boys do not communicate in the same way, or to the same extent as girls. Males tend to be more competitive and suppress emotions. One of the basic levels of MAT, if males are to behave in an anti-sexist way in what is an unequal society, is to recognize that such characteristics, for instance appearing tough and resolute, are products of conditioning, and not innate.

Implementation of equal opportunities policies This conditioning may cause problems when it comes to implementing equal opportunity policies. Local authorities have often been the first to introduce equal opportunity policies, to recognize the problem, and to develop principles and experience in the delivery of male awareness training. For instance, they have discovered through practice that the male trainers involved must have a personal commitment to the concept of equal opportunities, that consultations with relevant women's groups within the authority should take place to ensure the MAT's aims and objectives are understood, and that the training programme is ongoing, and not a series of 'one-offs'.

Male trainers The argument goes that the trainers should be male so that the male participants can explore their sexism in a secure situation. It also encourages the men to take responsibility for changing their attitudes. They must discover and understand the conditioning they have been subjected to, supported by the male trainers.

Consultations with women's groups Often women's groups feel anxious that if men are involved in training other men inequalities and attitudes are likely to be perpetuated rather than changed. But MAT is more than getting males to work in an anti-sexist way: it is aimed at developing an understanding of why they are sexist.

Ongoing training Once MAT becomes an accepted part of mainstream training, consideration should be given to the following issues:

- its implementation within departmental structures;
- whether participation should be compulsory or voluntary;
- its future development.

MAT should work as part of an equal opportunities policy, and as such has to be supported by senior management. Once this support is given, key officers can be instructed to attend a male awareness training course. Once a pilot course has been run, acceptance and development of a MAT programme becomes easier, and voluntary participation, which produces better results, should be the chosen method of recruitment. The next developmental stage should be for groups to cooperate to create and develop agreed anti-sexist working strategies and practice which should be monitored, evaluated and reviewed.

Campaigns to Increase Equality of Opportunity

Who should attend? Human resource managers and trainers interested and involved in joining national campaigns to increase the profile of an organization's equality programme.

By the end of the training programme delegates will have:

- gained an insight into the various programmes that are available, their purpose and how to join them;
- become familiar with the aims and activities of any specific programme of interest to them as individuals or as representatives of their parent organization.

A training programme should aim to cover the following information as a minimum:

Companies Act! Business Charter

A charter banning discrimination against people with AIDS or the HIV virus was launched in July 1992 by the charity National AIDS

Trust, with the support of almost twenty top British companies. National Westminster Bank, Body Shop, Rothschilds and Midland Bank are among those companies to have signed up to the Companies Act! Business Charter, pledging themselves to the 'principle of non-discrimination' when dealing with employees who have AIDS or HIV. The impetus for the charter has come from cases brought to the attention of the Trust where people with AIDS or HIV have lost their jobs either through direct or indirect discrimination by their employers. Why sign?

- the fight against AIDS,
- recognition as a good employer,
- educating employees,
- reassuring employees,
- public restatement of policy,
- encouraging good management.

Department for Employment's Equal Opportunities Ten Point Plan for Employers

The ten points for action are:

1 To develop an equal opportunities policy, embracing recruitment, promotion and training.
2 To set an action plan including targets, so that you and your staff have a clear idea of what can be achieved and by when.
3 To provide training for all to help people, including management, throughout your organization to understand the importance of equal opportunities, and provide additional training for staff who recruit, select and train your employees.
4 To monitor the present position to establish your starting point, and monitor progress in achieving objectives to identify successes and shortfalls.
5 To review recruitment, selection, promotion and training procedures regularly, to ensure that good intentions are being put into practice.
6 To draw up clear and justifiable job criteria and ensure these are objective and job-related.
7 To offer pre-employment training, where appropriate, to prepare potential job applicants for selection tests and interviews, and positive action training to help underrepresented groups.
8 To consider your organization's image; do you encourage applications from underrepresented groups, and feature women, ethnic minority staff and people with disabilities in recruitment literature, or could you be seen as an employer who marginalizes these groups?

9   To consider flexible working, career breaks, provision of childcare facilities, etc. to help women in particular meet domestic responsibilities and pursue their occupations; and the provision of special equipment and assistance to help people with disabilities.

10   To develop links with local community groups, organizations and schools, and so reach out to a wider pool of potential recruits.

Employers' Agenda on Disability – Ten Points for Action

In 1992, the Employers' Forum on Disability launched an Employers' Agenda on Disability – Ten Points for Action, to promote the recognition, recruitment and career development of people with disabilities. The agenda is backed by twenty-one leading UK employers including Anglia Television, B&Q, Barclays Bank, Boots, British Rail, National Westminster Bank and the Post Office, all of whom are members of the Forum. It also has the support of the Prime Minister, John Major. The twenty-one companies who have agreed to support the initiative will build the points for action into their equal opportunities policies. It is the first step to creating a blueprint for best practice, which the companies intend to promote throughout the business community. The key elements of the agenda are:

• Making a positive effort to attract people with disabilities and, once employed, to develop their careers to the benefit of the companies and the individuals themselves.
• Changing attitudes within the workplace through training and awareness programmes.
• Monitoring progress in implementing the agenda through an annual audit of performance, reviewed at board level. Achievements and objectives will be communicated to employers and published in UK annual reports.

The members of the Employers' Forum on Disability are working to create increasing opportunities for disabled people within their own companies. Historically, the concept of equal opportunities has been influenced by the legislation focused on women and ethnic minorities, while people with disabilities have been overlooked. Only 36 per cent of disabled men and 31 per cent of disabled women are in employment. These figures represent an enormous waste of talent and resources. Very often, employers simply do not know what needs to be done to undo the effects of discriminatory behaviour and patterns. The ten points for action are:

1   *Equal opportunities policy and procedures statement*   The employment of people with disabilities will form an integral part of all equal opportunities policies and practices.

2   *Staff training and disability awareness*   The company will take specific measures to raise awareness of disability throughout the organization.

3   *The working environment*   The company will take all reasonable steps to ensure the working environment does not prevent disabled people from taking up positions for which they are suitably qualified.

4   *Recruitment*   The company will review and develop recruitment procedures which encourage applications from people with disabilities.

5   *Career development*   The company will take specific steps to ensure that disabled people have the same opportunity as other staff to develop their full potential within the organization.

6   *Retention, retraining and redeployment*   Any employee who becomes disabled will be given the fullest support to return to a role appropriate to his or her experience and ability within the organization.

7   *Training and work experience*   The company will ensure that disabled people are involved in work experience and education/industry links as well as all forms of vocational training which are appropriate.

8   *People with disabilities in the wider community*   The company will respond to disabled people as customers, suppliers, shareholders, and members of the wider community in general.

9   *Involvement of disabled people*   When implementing the ten points for action, the company will encourage the full participation of disabled employees to ensure that employment practices reflect and meet their needs.

10   *Monitoring performance*   The company will monitor its progress in implementing the ten key points. There will be an annual audit of performance which will be reviewed at board level.

For further information on joining the Employers' Agenda for Disability contact the Employers' Forum on Disability (see address in appendix 1). The Forum is a non-profit-making organization funded by its fifty member companies, and works in association with the Prince of Wales' Advisory Group on Disability.

Government Childcare Initiative

Employers who are serious about recruiting and retaining women, and also allowing fathers to fulfil their parental responsibilities, are now thinking about how they can help their employees with childcare, as well as offering them the option of flexible working, job sharing and career breaks. In 1993 the government announced a 45 million pound initiative to stimulate an expansion of out-of-school childcare. It will support set-up costs for an additional 50,000 places in play schemes, child-minding or other care facilities. The funds are available from April 1993 for Training and Enterprise Councils (TECs) in England and Wales, and Local Enterprise Companies (LECs) in Scotland to work with a range of groups including:

- employers;
- schools;
- parents;
- local authorities;
- voluntary organizations;
- partnerships that want to set up out-of-school care.

The idea is that groups or individuals who want to start a scheme would go to their local TEC or LEC for advice from a development officer on obtaining training in business skills and possibly for help with start-up costs.

New Horizons for Women Initiative

In January 1993 the UK government launched the New Horizons for Women Initiative. This nationwide initiative aims to make people more aware of the fuller role that women can play and the range of opportunities available to them. The theme of the New Horizons for Women Initiative is that there are opportunities for all women, whatever their circumstances and aspirations. Although some women have managed to break the glass ceiling, overall they continue to be underrepresented in many areas of employment and public life. The campaign aims to highlight the message that there are opportunities for all women in many spheres such as:

- in employment;
- in training and education;
- in public life;
- in the voluntary sector.

For those women who have spent time away from the workplace bringing up a family or looking after an elderly or disabled relative, a return-to-work course may help to restore the confidence and skills they need to make that first step back. In March 1992 the Prime Minister asked individual government departments to formulate plans and set goals to increase the numbers of women appointed to government posts. They include:

- health authorities;
- consumer committees;
- employment and rent tribunals;
- research councils;
- the Board of the BBC.

By November 1992 the number of public appointments held by women had increased by 3 per cent to 26 per cent of the overall figure.

Opportunity 2000

Opportunity 2000 is about:

- promoting awareness of equality for women;
- demonstrating the potential of women;
- training staff;
- giving member firms an 'equality' backup.

Opportunity 2000 is a self-financing campaign launched in the UK in the autumn of 1991 and supported by the Prime Minister, who announced his personal commitment to recruit more women into top-level government positions. It has been established as the result of work carried out by the Women's Economic Development Team, chaired by Lady Howe and set up by the charity Business in the Community (BITC). The campaign aims to encourage British industry to take full advantage of the economic potential of women. It emphasizes that equal opportunities at work constitutes good economic as well as common sense, without ignoring the humanitarian nature of good equality practice. It is a unique approach to improvements in equality of opportunity in the UK. Founder members included:

- major banks and building societies;
- major high-street retailers;
- government departments;
- the police;
- educational establishments;
- major engineering companies;

- most of the UK's recently privatized large employers;
- publishers and television companies.

The Opportunity 2000 approach involves three key steps:

1 A public statement of commitment about an organization's special goals in the context of Opportunity 2000, and regular reporting of progress in annual reports.
2 An active ongoing programme of organized reform to provide a full range of equal opportunities. Improvements which are introduced will be measured to facilitate effective evaluation of equal opportunity policy and practice.
3 The development of goals and targets based on a participating organization's existing situation and assessment of future needs.

European Union Measures

Who should attend?

- first-time managers and middle managers, as the European equality ingredient in early management training;
- human resource managers with responsibility for staff development and training;
- training managers and trainers;
- equal opportunities specialists, experts and consultants;
- experienced managers to build a more productive and empowered team to take products, services and personnel into EU markets.

By the end of the training programme delegates will have:

- learned about the major EU equality measures and how to access programmes of interest to themselves or to their organizations;
- developed, rehearsed and evaluated different methods of incorporating a more European bias into their equality programmes.

A training programme should aim to cover the following information as a minimum:

The EU has introduced laws and action programmes to promote equal opportunities. Within the field of equality its measures focus on sex discrimination, age and disability. Little has been achieved in promoting equality and non-discrimination on the grounds of race and sexuality. To date the European Commission has adopted five Directives on equality of opportunity for men and women. European law on equal treatment between men and women consists of Article 119 of the Treaty of Rome which states that men and women should receive equal pay for equal work, and five equality Directives. Directives have the force of the law; the EU decides what must happen but leaves it to member states to introduce national laws to comply with the Directive. The five Directives are:

1 The equal pay Directive.
2 The Directive on equal treatment in employment, which has banned all sex-based discrimination at work.
3 The social security Directive, which is aimed at achieving equal treatment for women and men in social security schemes.
4 The Directive on occupational social security schemes, which extends the rule of equal treatment in social security to include occupational social security schemes.
5 The Directive for the self-employed relates to the provision of equal treatment for women who are self-employed, or who work entirely or part with their spouses.

At the end of 1991 the European Commission agreed to adopt a Directive on pregnancy at work. From 1994 pregnant women throughout the European Union qualify for up to fourteen weeks maternity leave irrespective of their length of service with their employer.

The European Commission's action programmes

Equal Opportunities for women 1991–1995 (A similar extended programme is expected to run from 1996–2000.) This action is the third of its kind and lays down three main courses of action:

• to apply the legal framework under the equality Directives so that equal opportunities for women becomes a fact rather than just a legal right on paper;
• to promote the integration of women into all sectors of paid employment;
• to improve the status of women in society.

Disability The HELIOS programme is to run 1992–6. It stands for Handicapped People Living Independently in an Open Society. The programme's aims include:

- ongoing development of vocational training centres;
- financial help towards the cost of adapting premises to accommodate handicapped people, for instance, by constructing ramps for wheelchair access, lifts, hoists, ground floor toilets and kitchen facilities;
- start-up assistance for schemes designed to increase the number of people with disabilities in useful employment. In practice this can include a whole range of special aids and equipment, such as a personal reader service for employees with a visual handicap.

Older people　In 1991, an EU action programme for older people was launched. The launch focused on a range of subjects including the social integration of older people and their right to independent living. The Commission has agreed to set up an information system on organizations and schemes throughout Europe which are concerned with the needs of older people. This will help in the exchange of ideas and the sharing of good practice between member states. Also, 1993 was nominated the European Year of the Elderly, and measures to assist older people in a whole range of ways have been developed throughout the European Union. Information on all of the equality programmes within the EU can be obtained from the European Commission or from Age Concern.

The Bureau for Questions concerning Employment and Equal Treatment for Women

The bureau implements EU policy on equal treatment. It monitors the application of existing Directives in every member state. It ensures that the principle of equal treatment is taken into account in other EU policies, for example, education, training or business development programmes for small businesses. It promotes positive action in firms and organizes or supports a variety of activities in the field of women's rights. For further information contact:

> The Commission of the European Communities Directorate-General 5
> Bureau for Questions concerning Employment and Equal Treatment for Women
> 200 rue de la Loi
> 1049 Brussels
> Belgium
> Tel: 101 322 2353032

The Advisory Committee on Equal Opportunities for Men and Women

This committee advises the European Commission on drafting its equal opportunities policies and promotes the exchange of experience between Member States. It is composed of representatives working with equal opportunities issues in the Member States.

The Information Unit for Women

The task of this unit is to inform female opinion. It maintains a regular dialogue with women's interest organizations. The unit produces a bi-monthly newsletter called *Women in Europe* giving news of equal opportunities developments in community policy and national laws. For more information contact:

> The Commission of the European Communities
> Directorate-General for Information, Communication and
>   Culture
> Information for Women Division
> 200 rue de la Loi
> 1049 Brussels
> Belgium

Forming and Implementing an Equal Opportunities Policy

Who should attend?

- human resource managers with specific as well as general duties concerned with developing, maintaining and improving equal opportunities measures;
- equal opportunities specialists and trainers;
- departmental managers with responsibilities to develop policy in their areas;
- everyone – so that they can feel comfortable in dealing with one another, work together more productively and understand and apply the equal opportunities policy.

By the end of the training delegates will have:

- analysed and discussed the purpose of an equal opportunities policy;
- gained an appreciation of what should be included in an equal opportunities policy;

- examined ways of turning policy into practice;
- looked at the purpose and methods behind policy review, monitoring and evaluation.

A training programme should aim to cover the following information as a minimum:

An early step in implementing a policy for equal opportunities in employment is to examine existing personnel procedures and practices to assess whether, and to what extent, they safeguard and promote equality of opportunity. The review should cover all aspects of an organization's recruitment, selection, promotion and training processes. If it is discovered that practices or requirements are unfair, potentially unlawful, unnecessary, or unjustifiably exclude or limit opportunities for certain groups, they should be changed or discontinued.

Constituents of an equal opportunities policy:

- An equal opportunities policy must address prejudice and discrimination separately, as well as both direct and indirect discrimination. An organization's response to each should acknowledge that they are separate conditions.
- A statement of intent to avoid discrimination, and to challenge it if, or when, it occurs.
- What it means in terms of recruitment, selection and promotion procedures, and training.
- How the policy will be monitored and who will be responsible for it.
- In an integrated policy, mention must be made of all discriminators in the form of clear and concise definitions of each, to ensure that staff can obtain the information they need about company practice without having to ask specific questions.
- Any policy must state clearly that discrimination in any aspect of company activity against anyone who is HIV positive or has AIDS will not be tolerated.
- A clear statement about confidentiality, explaining the ways in which confidential information will be treated.
- What it means in terms of discipline and grievance procedures; what action will be taken if staff breach the terms laid down.

The best model policies will also cover areas such as:

- opportunities for redeployment or retraining;
- flexible working arrangements;

- parental leave and parental rights;
- compassionate leave, etc.

*Steps to be taken to ensure the successful implementation of an
equal opportunities policy:*

1 Elect a person to be responsible.
2 Provide training.
3 Ensure that all employees know about the policy.
4 Examine existing policies and practices to ensure that they are not contrary to equal opportunities.
5 Form an equal opportunities working party made up of members from each section and all grades.
6 Allow specific time to implement, monitor and review the policy.
7 Foster effective internal communication and external relations.
8 Introduce positive action measures and good practices developed elsewhere and adopted by equality network members.

Monitoring and Evaluation in Developing Equality of Opportunity

Who should attend?

- human resource managers involved in equal opportunities development and review;
- middle managers and supervisors;
- equal opportunities specialists.

By the end of a training programme delegates will have:

- appreciated the meaning and purpose of monitoring and evaluation;
- explored and developed appropriate methods for their own organizations.

A training programme should aim to cover the following information as a minimum:

Monitoring is perhaps the single most important issue which organizations need to address if they are to make progress on equal opportunities issues. It is evident that no convincing equal opportunities strategy with measurable targets can be effective unless progress towards those issues is measured and analysed, and attempts made to adjust performance in light of the monitoring feedback. Without effective monitoring an organization:

- cannot be sure that it is achieving its strategic objectives in the equal opportunities field;
- cannot identify and reward those of its managers and training providers who are making progress;
- cannot take remedial action for those who are not;
- cannot promote (and indeed defend) its approach towards equality of opportunity to its local community.

What is effective monitoring?

The principles of effective monitoring of equal opportunities policy are well established. Originally developed for the monitoring of equal opportunities within employing organizations, the principles apply equally with regard to training and enterprise programmes, and there is general agreement on the kinds of data which are required as a minimum (although there has been some debate about which are the most appropriate ethnic categories to use). The data necessary for effective monitoring are, moreover, the same kinds of data which would be required for normal management information purposes. It is difficult to see how many organizations could meet their requirements for effective quality systems audits without such data. Effective monitoring for equal opportunities purposes involves three data processes about training programmes and participants:

- collation;
- analysis;
- feedback.

The data are captured through a regular and systematic process. At a minimum this is likely to be:

- on entry to a training programme;
- on exit from a training programme.

Intermediate stages of data capture may also be appropriate in some situations. Ideally this information is input to a computerized management information system, which allows both the production of the kinds of aggregated data required for managerial or board of director purposes, for example, and the more detailed data necessary to monitor an organization's own training programmes run by internal training providers as well as those run by external trainers. The Commission for Racial Equality have produced *TECs, LECs and Training: A Guide To Equality Audits*, which sets out in clear terms some of the main principles underlying equal opportunities monitoring and the data required. The CRE guide concentrates on race, but the principles and processes are the same with regards to monitoring sex and disability issues and any monitoring process would normally aim simultaneously to capture information relating to all forms of equal opportunities target groups.

The elements of monitoring

Key elements of any monitoring system are likely to involve a number of steps.

Data collection at point of entry   Organizations will need to decide for themselves the minimum data they require, bearing in mind the following four factors:

- the requirements of the board of directors;
- the demands of training providers;
- the requirements of any external bodies such as local authorities, examination boards or campaign requirements such as those of Opportunity 2000;
- their own monitoring needs.

At a minimum, this is likely to include basic data and individual characteristics relevant to equal opportunities at the point of entry to the programme. These are:

- sex;
- ethnicity;
- disability classification;
- age;
- position or grade in company.

The more detail provided about the classification of disability and race the better, given the varied needs and problems of the different groups. Ideally it will also include some of the data on individual personal characteristics, for example:

- prior qualifications;
- current employment and employment history;
- residential post-code (the latter can be particularly important for ethnic monitoring, given the geographical concentration of many minority groups).

Data on the particular training programme being entered is also important for monitoring purposes, especially in large organizations. At a minimum this will identify:

- the training provider;
- the occupational area of training.

Ideally the process should also collect information on applicants who are not accepted for the programme, which can be crucial in investigating the causes of any systematic underrepresentation of particular groups on the programme. (For example, is it because these groups do not apply for the programme, perhaps because of inadequate/poorly targeted marketing, or is it that they do apply but are not chosen by the provider?) In practice, however, it is recognized that to extend monitoring systems in this way would be a major task for many organizations.

Data collection at point of exit from a training programme (and intermediate points if appropriate)   A monitoring system must be designed so that this information can be linked with the start information on an individual basis. The ability to undertake tracking at an individual level is crucial for any diagnosis of problems that are revealed at an aggregate level. If this linking is done, then the data set is a 'cohort' rather than two 'cross-sections', and information does not need to be re-collected about those characteristics which will not have changed from entry, or which can be inferred from the entry information (sex, race, age, etc.). The date of leaving is clearly important, as is the outcome or destination of a training participant, and any qualifications gained.

Data analysis   At a minimum this looks at entry/participation rates of different groups on different programmes, and the relative performance of those groups on leaving the programmes (in terms of outcomes, durations, and other performance indicators which an organization uses).

Assessment   Having conducted the analysis, some baseline or benchmark will be required against which an organization can assess whether performance is good or bad. Normally, for participation rates, this will involve at least a comparison with the representation in the relevant population from which the eligible group is drawn. It is important to assess the definition of the relevant group correctly. For example, the incidence of disability varies with age, and it would be inappropriate to compare the proportion of young people who are disabled with the proportion of disabled people in the population as a whole. Similarly crucial, in a case of ethnic monitoring, is a definition of the relevant geographical area from which the relevant population is drawn. When outcomes are being examined, the comparison will normally be between the various groups participating in the programme. Trainers should be aware of two potential factors:

- Do white participants consistently get better outcomes than those from ethnic minorities?
- Do male participants fare better than female?

Each organization is likely to wish to set regular targets against which to monitor progress:

- In the case of participation rates, targets are likely to be drawn from the representation in the relevant population in question.
- In the case of outcomes, targets are likely to be set in terms of progress towards equality of outcomes for the different groups.

An important choice for each organization is to decide the level at which the targeting and subsequent managing takes place. For example:

- it could be done at the level of whole programmes,
- at the level of occupational categories,
- at the level of individual providers.

Organizations are likely to need to monitor to at least the second of these levels – it is important to check not only whether women and ethnic minorities are adequately represented in a programme as a whole, but also whether they are concentrated in particular types of training. In the case of women in particular, it is clear that 'occupational segregation' is one of the main equal opportunities issues that relates to training provision.

Feedback and review Finally, the process involves feedback and review of the monitoring assessments with the following people:

- managers;
- staff;
- training providers;
- others responsible for improving performance against set targets.

This essential part of the managerial process will vary between organizations. It will, for example, be important to take account of how far failure to achieve targets reflects changes in the external labour market and the organization's or the provider's inability to influence it. The only general point which can be made is that any effective monitoring system will involve such a feedback and review stage, with the key actors involved, on a regular basis.

Sharing systems expertise

Few organizations are at the stage of being able to conduct fully effective equal opportunities monitoring of their programmes and providers, and it is understandable that having struggled, and in many cases having abandoned the struggle, some organizations are unenthusiastic at the thought of developing new monitoring systems. Given, however, that some organizations are further down the road than others in this respect, there is an important case for sharing existing expertise. It is not inconceivable that some organizations will be happy to recoup some of their investment costs in this area, while others will be willing to pay to avoid the time/cost involved in reinventing the wheel.

Networking: Working with Others

Who should attend?

- First line and middle managers, particularly in their dealings with colleagues in other departments and with outside agencies.
- Professionals and experts in the equality field. (The rules of hierarchy do not apply in the majority of equality situations; subtler methods of communication such as networking have to be used.)
- Salespeople negotiating with customers and clients: the techniques used have to be compatible with an organization's equality philosophy.
- Secretarial and clerical staff. Their effectiveness depends a great deal on their ability to get on with others in a productive way and network among other departments and organizations.

By the end of the training programme delegates will have:

- become familiar with the principles of networking;
- been introduced to examples of effective real-life networking situations;
- explored situations related to their own work that could be improved by setting up or linking into an existing network;

- explored different methods of communication that are best applied to different situations;
- understood the need to communicate assertively and accurately;
- understood the benefits of sharing information through effective networking and avoiding the duplication of effort and resources through singular isolated projects;
- learned techniques of handling day-to-day networking;
- formed an action plan to implement all the learning gained during the course.

Training programmes should aim to cover the following information as a minimum:

Networking begins with informal exchanges, provided that these exchanges have some merit. Unlike rigid training courses, the main feature of networking is the constant adjustment of the 'curriculum' to the needs of the participants. Networks aim to combine economic efficiency with social interaction at work. Working within networks helps encourage employees:

- to accept responsibility;
- to identify with company aims;
- to participate in company life.

They also help to foster cooperation and improve the working climate. Numerous examples show that effective networking improves communication, so enhancing customer service as well as management and management methods. Bringing down costs while improving cooperation is ideally suited to achieving company aims while simultaneously realizing every participant's potential. In short, employees with greater trust and self-confidence form the bedrock for increased productivity.

While not neglecting the general aspects which always form part of this type of training (talks, summaries, meetings, etc.), the work is set with regard to the individual needs of each member. Most networking exercises are halfway between the fields of self-expression and creativity. Networking groups work interactively. The roles are distributed in such a way that listening is just as important as self-expression. The approach is supplemented by encouraging the students to read relevant material and suggest topics for future meetings and debate. Networking has a triple value:

- it stimulates creativity by helping participants to discover their way of expressing themselves;
- it offers them an opportunity to assimilate and disseminate information jointly;
- it offers them a chance to reproduce information in a time- and resource-efficient manner.

The European networks of innovative projects involving older people aim to facilitate and stimulate the exchange of information and experience at a practical level and to provide models and knowledge for interested parties and practitioners including those outside the networks. Some examples are given below.

Seniorama

Seniorama aims to help elderly persons to be fully accepted by and integrated into society. Its methods are based on a tripartite picture of community work:

- problems are tackled in consultation with senior citizens;
- solutions are sought which take account of each individual's own situation;
- participants are given a greater sense of responsibility and self-motivation.

Elderly persons, volunteers, management and staff work together with the aim of improving the quality of life of the residents.

Contact: M. M. Herregodts
Seniorama
Munstraat 13
B-3000 Leuven

The 'Antenne Andromede'

This project was designed for able-bodied elderly people who wish to combat loneliness while retaining their independence. Six flats are available in a social housing area and contain communal as well as private areas. Members live together in a residential situation. The groups are formed by mutual selection. After a series of meetings potential residents select the groups with whom they want to live.

Contact: C. P. A. S. de Woluwe-St-Lambert
Rue de la Charette 27
B-1200 Brussels

Social Community Project

The idea of a social community is an attempt to structure social policy at municipal level in a way that will encourage the broadest possible interaction between those concerned. These include:

- academic experts;
- financiers;
- professional associations and organizations;
- advisers in gerontology;
- self-help groups.

It concentrates on shifting the coordination of administration of local authority age welfare policy onto an interdepartmental basis. An age policy coordination centre has been set up for this purpose.

Contact: Herr Borosch
Ministerium fur Arbeit
Gesundheit und Soziales des Nordrhein-Westfahlen
Horizonplatz 1
D-4000 Dusseldorf

Sheltered Group Living Scheme

The scheme comprises a single house based in an ordinary community where three elderly people live together, share the same home and support each other. A paid worker goes in every day, the amount of care provided depends on the particular needs of each individual in the home. The scheme allows elderly people to remain within the community, retaining considerable independence, with the support they need. Since the support provided can be tailored to their particular needs, it is particularly suited to respond to specialized needs, including those of black and racial minority groups.

Contact: Mr R. Currie
Liverpool Personal Service Society
18-28 Seel Street
Liverpool
L1 4BE
United Kingdom

Calderdale Travelling Day Hospital

The Travelling Day Hospital team provides assessment, treatment and support to elderly people with mental problems and their carers.

It works on the basis of an open referral system; patients may be referred by health professionals or by self-referral. Each client referred receives a comprehensive assessment undertaken by the team. The team liaises with statutory and voluntary agencies towards the provision of streamlined care.

Contact: Mr John Ketteringham
            Senior Clinical Nurse
            Northowram Hospital
            Halifax
            HX1 1UJ
            United Kingdom

Positive Action

Who should attend?

- human resource managers interested in developing positive action measures;
- equal opportunities committee or working party members;
- staff interested in developing and attending positive action courses;
- everyone – so that they can feel comfortable in dealing with one another and work together more productively.

What should a positive action course do?

- encourage collaboration between different kinds of groups;
- help non-traditional employees get integrated and promoted;
- defuse conflict in the workplace by increasing awareness of equality enhancement through positive action initiatives;
- handle sensitive issues in a non-threatening way.

By the end of the training programme delegates will have:

- understood what is meant by positive action and how it can be applied;
- appreciated the reasons for developing positive action measures;
- explored ways of developing and implementing positive action training measures in their own organizations, departments and teams;
- examined various positive action methods and determined which methods to adopt according to the situation;
- formed a plan of action to implement all the learning gained during the course.

Training programmes should aim to cover the following information as a minimum:

What is positive action?

Positive action is about the provision of equal opportunities in employment. It is sometimes incorrectly referred to as positive discrimination. Both the Sex Discrimination Act and the Race Relations Act allow certain forms of positive action. The main purpose of positive action is to undo the effects of past race and sex discrimination. Training organizations, employers, and trade unions may take positive action measures to encourage members of a particular group to take advantage of opportunities for participating in jobs within a particular department. The Employment Act of 1989 has broadened the scope of the Race Relations Act and positive action training can now be provided by anyone. Examples of positive action in recruitment might include:

* the placing of job advertisements in ethnic minority newspapers to attract black applicants;
* the use of employment agencies and careers offices in areas where high numbers of ethnic minorities live, for example, Toxteth in Liverpool and Handsworth in Birmingham.

Positive action is not only a UK-based initiative. The USA has a long-established system of affirmative action, and several EU states have equivalent schemes designed to improve equal opportunities. In order to improve positive action in the workplace it is essential that all companies first become equal opportunities employers. An equal opportunities policy and statement of good intention are important starting points to achieve total commitment to equality. Positive action also helps focus on traditionally held assumptions about what are men's and women's jobs, and the type of experience which is really necessary to fill such jobs. For example, it may well be customary to fill middle management posts from the technical department of a company which is predominantly male, rather than from the administrative and secretarial section which is predominantly female, even though their experience is probably as relevant. Positive action schemes should develop training programmes designed to compensate women for past discrimination. Similarly, equivalent measures to promote ethnic minorities need to be more widely developed in the majority of companies.

Positive action programmes in the EU

As part of the EU Directive on equal opportunities for women a number of new action programmes are planned. Many other programmes have been running successfully since the early 1980s. New Opportunities for Women (NOW) is an EU-led programme which has been designed to undo the effects of inequality between men and women in the labour market. It has also placed increased pressure on national governments to comply with the principle of 'equal pay for work of equal value' laid down in the Treaty of Rome. EU positive action measures aimed at abolishing the discrimination experienced by workers with disability are also being adopted. HELIOS is an EU-led action programme designed to promote disabled workers in the labour market and raise employers' awareness of the ability and capacity of disabled people, to counter the negative prejudice about disability.

Why?

In order to implement a successful positive action programme that promotes women, black people, employees with disabilities or older workers inside a company, human resource managers have to be convinced of the validity of this action and know how to convince others, particularly company directors and top management. Thus, they need to be completely persuaded of the legitimate reasons for the project and be able to develop convincing arguments.

A major reason is to put into practice a policy of equal opportunities in employment The following are recognized principles in all EU member countries: non-discrimination, either direct or indirect, against women in employment; the equal treatment of men and women in matters of training, employment and social protection as recommended in the 1976 Directive; equal opportunities to combat indirect forms of discrimination. However, the unequal employment situation of men and women is a recognized, statistically proven fact:

- there are proportionately more women working in insecure, temporary or part-time jobs;
- their jobs are less diverse and often less skilled than those of men;
- they do not benefit from in-company training as much as men;
- women are less familiar with technical innovations;
- on the whole, women earn less than men working in the same field;

- they are more rarely and more slowly promoted;
- there are proportionately fewer women in jobs of responsibility;
- there is a higher unemployment rate among women in eleven out of twelve EU countries.

A policy of equal opportunities must put into practice the principles for changing this unjust reality by:

- identifying the areas and causes of inequality;
- defining a strategy to fight against the discrimination, attitudes and barriers to progress which perpetuate this situation;
- setting up a structure within a company which ensures that this strategy is permanently applied.

Other reasons of the same kind:

- In addition to EU Directives, several states have adopted equality plans for women in employment. A positive action programme in favour of women in a company is a real application of these provisions.
- In some member states, there is still little information on the situation of women in the workforce, as many employment statistics are not drawn up according to sex, or the data are incomplete and the situation of women is only known in certain fields of activity or in certain state establishments, or the data are limited. If we are to know more about the real situation of women in employment, then it is important to carry out research inside companies to obtain information regarding different posts and grades, the salary scale, training and promotion organized by the company, and so on.

An attractive reason for companies is that positive action is the practical application of a policy which maximizes human resources in the company. Faced with technological change affecting production, company organization and management, an increasing number of public and private enterprises are concerned to know more about and make better use of their human resources. Cutting out jobs that are obsolete and laying off staff, and recruiting new or recently trained personnel for newly created posts is a very costly solution; it also risks damaging the company spirit, creating a bad internal atmosphere, and cannot be sustained throughout the whole period of change. Hence, the interest shown by top companies in making the most of their existing personnel. This problem occurs to a greater extent in companies that employ a high number of women because:

- it is very often women who occupy the jobs which disappear with technological change;
- women are often the least well-known members of the personnel (in terms of their employment potential) because, until now, set attitudes towards women's work mean that they are often recruited and maintained in routine jobs, without any real further investigation into their different capabilities;
- female staff with no future, who often feel overqualified for their jobs, become uninterested in the progress of the company and harbour feelings of bitterness, resulting in a staff turnover higher than the norm.

Consequently, the organization of interviews and internal assessments which open up the possibility of career development for women and encourage them to do further training would be beneficial for many organizations. Companies which appreciate these reasons may devise positive action programmes differently according to their general organization. Those in which nearly all the administrative staff are women will give these women priority – especially since new technology has revolutionized the traditional office jobs of switchboard operator, secretary, etc. Production companies which use female labour may carry out action aimed at enabling them to redeploy successfully their unskilled female staff in the face of technology change; without such positive action measures, these women could be laid off and replaced by more highly skilled men.

Public sector businesses cannot fail to be aware of their moral obligation to apply the EU equality plans adopted or recommended by their government; such is the case of ministerial departments, regional administrations, or large state-owned companies, for example, telecommunications, radio, television, public health, banks, and so on.

There are several other reasons why positive action should be promoted within organizations. These include:

- The company will know more about the potential and ambitions of its female staff; also of frustrations and hidden problems.
- Women employees will be better informed about the aims, organization and development obligations of the company, and will feel more integrated and motivated.
- They will probably be absent less often, and will be more efficient and creative in their jobs, more willing to communicate their ideas and to work as part of a team.

- Organizations will be more rational and flexible than when there are hidden sexist barriers, women will be employed according to their level, authoritarian 'petty bosses' will no longer impede change.
- The public image of a company will be very much improved; it can advertise the fact that it offers equal opportunities to women in accordance with EU Directives and that it is ready for a united Europe.
- Union relations will be very much improved, especially if the unions take an active role in the programme. The company will improve its credibility; it shows that it has nothing to hide and that it is able to question and change its policies.

For whom?

Obviously, positive action programmes are for improving the situation of women or other disadvantaged groups employed in a particular company. However, the advantages of such action may well be more far-reaching and benefit all disadvantaged groups working in similar companies in the same branch or sector. For example, where collective agreements in a particular branch of industry are modified or enhanced as a result of a positive action programme, companies in competition may imitate the action. If a company receives radio or television coverage because of its equal opportunities plan for women, then one or more competitors may well follow the example to avoid being labelled as reactionary.

The types of companies in which action programmes might be implemented

- Companies from the service industries which employ a high number of women, are in full expansion, and in which new technology has had and continues to have an important impact. The industries involved in these processes include: financial establishments such as banks, savings banks and insurance companies; large property management firms; large travel agents; and clinics and hospitals.
- Industrial manufacturing companies which employ a large number of women and are undergoing technological change: textiles, clothing, electronics, food, cosmetics, pharmaceuticals, etc.
- Administrative services in which the jobs held by women are not very diverse: regional, provincial and municipal administrations, finance, tax and customs departments, etc.
- State-owned or formerly state-owned companies in which the jobs held by women are not very diverse: national railways, radio and television, gas, electricity and water boards, urban transport, etc.

The categories of women that need to be helped

- women trapped in jobs which hold no future and who stand no chance of moving without positive action aid;
- women employed in offices to do the bookkeeping, data processing, filing, typing, simple storekeeping, cleaning, etc.;
- women whose jobs are obsolete and who risk being laid off if they do not learn new skills;
- women graduates who are underemployed in view of their level of education because their course of study did not prepare them for employment and who need to be redeployed in more technical fields if they want a career commensurate with their level of education;
- women in middle management positions unable to obtain further promotion due to 'invisible barriers' (in reality sex discrimination) who stand a chance of moving up in the company with the help of positive action.

Other considerations when choosing a company for positive action

- from the point of view of publicity for the programme, it is a good idea to select one or more companies from a fairly prestigious sector, which is seen as being active, modern and open towards new technology;
- it is easier to carry out positive action in a large company which already has a well-defined staff policy;
- nevertheless, medium-sized companies may be very interested in such an action if they are undergoing complete reorganization, are certain to need extra qualified staff, and are concerned with economic efficiency.

With whom?

The company management is the main partner, particularly in the preliminary stage during which decisions are made concerning the aims and activities to take place. It is therefore essential to obtain as much information as possible on the company management beforehand, in order to prepare your positive action proposal and convincing arguments well. This information might include, for example:

- the financial situation of the company;
- the need for change (technological and organizational);
- details of the company 'culture';
- its background history.

Trainers need to meet the general manager or assistant general manager at least once at the company head office and/or obtain their personal support. Important contacts throughout the duration of a training programme are:

* personnel or human resources managers;
* those in charge of in-house training;
* those in charge of development and expansion;
* local branch or agency managers;
* the main department managers;
* in the case of industrial companies, those in charge of production.

Request at the first meeting that the company management appoint several members of the managerial staff to coordinate and be responsible for the action inside the company. They will keep in constant contact with you. It is preferable to make a distinction between the members of the *action committee* who have responsibility for the action programme, and those who are appointed by the action committee to participate in the *working party* set up to organize the running of the programme. Those employees appointed to the working party should be allowed specific time by the management to work on positive action measures.

The trade union or unions are sometimes the first associates as they may be approached for information even before choosing the branch of industry or company in which a positive action programme is to take place. Arrange to meet consecutively:

* the members of a trade union federation responsible for the situation of women, black people, disability issues, etc.;
* the members of a trade union for the particular branch or sector chosen – banking union, union for the chemical industry, hospitals, schools, engineering, etc.;
* the women's group affiliated to the union or unions involved – there is always a more or less official women's committee or group in charge of looking after the interests of women employed in that branch of industry.

There may be no union branch in the company where the action programme is being run. If this is the case, then contact should be made with the company employees' representatives who are requested to sit on the action committee and working party, and afterwards on the *permanent equal opportunities committee*. A close working relationship with non-unionized employees' representatives does not, however, replace the indispensable contact with the official unions of the particular branch of industry.

The national equal opportunities agency   The action often takes place under the aegis of this organization, with its financial and administrative assistance. Even if this is not the case, it must be kept constantly informed of the progress of the action programme. The regional or local Equality for Women representative is frequently an invaluable partner and should be involved throughout.

The regional, provincial or municipal administration or department may be an associate, if the project takes place in an administration service or state enterprise under their authority.

External assistance   may need to be sought in some cases, for example:

* to carry out specific tasks;
* to prepare and interpret the results of a questionnaire;
* to carry out detailed interviews;
* to assess the abilities and motivation of candidates for job change;
* to give talks on or to lead discussions on equal opportunities for women in employment;
* to train small groups in negotiation techniques, team work, career planning, etc.

These people need to be carefully selected for their absolute professional discretion and experience concerning the problems encountered by women in employment.

Towards what aim?

The final aim of positive action is to establish a company policy of equal opportunities for women which permanently guarantees one or more, or all, of the following:

* To diversify the jobs and posts held by women in the company. This is largely achieved by investigating the departments where there is a high majority of women employees to find out who would like to, and could, carry out other jobs in the company, particularly those occupations which hitherto have been mostly the preserve of males. This means opening up the 'female ghetto' departments and proving that women recruited for jobs traditionally considered to be women's jobs can, with the help of in-company training schemes, change their jobs within the

company and become valuable elements in areas where women were previously underrepresented.

- To balance the distribution of men and women in a maximum number of posts. The aim is for women to gain entry to occupations and departments previously dominated by men and vice versa. Also, to obtain a certain balance between men and women at different levels in the company hierarchy.
- To create conditions in which women who have previously been held back are able to demonstrate their skills, talents and potential abilities.
- To promote women to higher grades, including board and top management positions. The internal promotion system needs to be analysed and changed if there is too low a proportion of women receiving promotion. The top positions in a company should be equally accessible to men and women. It is important to find out why certain women do not apply for positions of responsibility. A minimum target for women to receive promotion should be fixed over a set period of time.
- To increase the number of women working in the company by introducing a recruitment policy which favours women at the levels where they are underrepresented. All recruitment policies should be used to redress any imbalances between men and women employed in different jobs and grades.
- To raise the awareness and increase the qualifications level of groups that are underrepresented at jobs above a certain level, mainly through in-company training and ensuring that a certain percentage of women are admitted on company training courses and that they apply for new jobs.
- To ensure that women are fully involved in technological progress. It has long been observed in the sociology of female labour that women are not generally put on new machines nor are they given immediate training in new methods. Today, we live in a fast-changing world and women need to be involved in all technological innovations.
- To institute a wages policy that does not disadvantage women. Studies of men's and women's total wages show that the bonus and overtime systems in many companies often disadvantage women. This form of hidden discrimination needs to be uncovered, so that more equitable wages policies can be established.
- To improve the working conditions of women in terms of safety and special health provision, particularly during and after pregnancy. To provide facilities which allow both men and women to make their family and working lives more compatible (hours, assistance with childcare and other services for children).

How?

The action team or its main representatives, together with the company management, set up an action committee. The functions of this committee are:

- To draw up a protocol agreement, to be signed by the action team representatives and company management, to define a number of key points, for example: stipulating who is responsible for what during the course of the positive action programme; defining the degree of freedom the action team is allowed in the company; defining the financial and legal aspects of the positive action programme; defining any issues of confidentiality about the information collected, including conditions of use for films, videos, photographs and recordings made during the action.
- To decide on a general plan of action based on proposals from the action team and observations made by the company management: in other words, it must decide on the aims of the action, the means and persons involved to achieve them, and an approximate timetable.
- To appoint the members of a working party active for the duration of the project. These include members of the project organizing team, company representatives chosen by the management and union representatives.
- To appoint the members of the permanent equal opportunities committee to remain in existence after the project to ensure that the chosen policy is applied. The committee will mainly be made up of company and union representatives who will have been active in the working party.

A working party is the main instrument of the action, and its role is to:

- Prepare the different stages of the project.
- Supervise the questionnaires and all investigation material prepared by the project organizing team.
- Supervise the analysis of the statistics on the distribution of men/women, black and ethnic minority staff and disabled staff, and the results of the questionnaires, detailed interviews, assessments, and all investigations carried out in the company by the action team.
- In view of all this information, decide on how the action is to be continued. The working party will therefore study the aims of the project more closely and consider how these are to be achieved both during and after the project.
- Ensure that permanent equal opportunities subcommittees are set up in each branch or main department of the company (if it is a very large company). These will be responsible for ensuring that decisions are carried out (abolition of discriminatory practices, improvement in working conditions, increase in proportions of women trained or promoted, etc.). These subcommittees should work in liaison with the permanent committee.

- Make regular evaluations of the positive action programme during the first year.
- Prepare outside publicity events, either inviting people from outside the company or holding the events outside the company. The working party should make a list of guests, speakers, etc.
- Supervise the printed (display boards, posters, brochures, etc.) and audiovisual (video, film, photographs for exhibitions, recordings) materials used for publicizing the project during publicity events and dissemination campaigns.

The methods used by the action organizing team mainly consist of:

- Critically analysing statistical data according to sex and race provided by the company. A very good knowledge of the company organization is needed to have a clear-sighted view of this information.
- Using questionnaires to carry out a survey among a sample group of people chosen by the working party. If the action team does not include a specialist in the design of questionnaires and their interpretation, it is best to appoint a professional psycho-sociologist from outside the company.
- Analysing detailed interviews and personal accounts.
- Organizing small discussion groups and seminars run by the action team for the company staff to make them aware of the aims of the action.
- Training women how to negotiate, take decisions, etc. Assisting them in improving their understanding of how the company operates and in developing a personal career plan.
- Making assessments of the professional experience, abilities, ambitions and motivations of women applicants for a change of post or promotion.
- Training company executives in equal opportunities. This may take the form of a residential seminar during which they will be shown how the sexual and racial prejudice mechanisms work by means of certain tests, role-play activities and studies of cases that have arisen in companies.

Procedures for Recruitment and for Selection for Promotion and Training

Who should attend? This programme will help anyone who manages others to relate equality principles and practices to human resource management situations. They will be able to identify specific steps to strengthen their own management abilities.

By the end of the training programme delegates will have:

- considered their role as managers and clarified the demands that are made on them, the constraints they work with and the choices they can make;
- learned techniques of selection and recruitment that take full account of equal opportunities law and policy;
- explored different methods of recruitment and decision making and thought about which are best applied to which situation;
- developed effective techniques to give positive and negative feedback to staff in light of their responsibilities under equality laws.

A training programme should aim to cover the following information as a minimum:

It is important to review recruitment, selection, promotion and training procedures regularly to ensure that good intentions are being put into practice. Each procedure has a fundamental effect on how an organization functions and progresses. Retaining and developing employees requires personnel practices which are not only effective but can be seen to be fair.

Benefits of good employment procedures   Employers who use fair practices and monitor them provide a positive environment within which employees can use and develop their abilities to the full for the benefit of the organization and themselves.

Benefits an organization can reap include:

In recruiting staff   Widening the recruitment net so that all sectors of the community have the opportunity to apply for vacancies improves an organization's chance of attracting the best candidate first time. This may also reduce recruitment costs.

In retaining staff   Enhancing morale and prospects can lead to a lower level of absenteeism and turnover, which in turn helps to reduce costs and maintain output.

For the business   Clear evidence that an organization is an equal opportunities employer projects a more positive image and promotes business growth.

Recruiting, selecting, training and promoting staff is a matching process. The aim must always be to select the most suitable person for the job or all those who can benefit most from a training course. It is therefore important that existing procedures are reviewed regularly, and changed if they fail to meet this principle. The key to a successful recruitment, selection, promotion and training process is the adoption of a systematic and objective approach.

Actions to consider:

- preparing clear job descriptions and updating them regularly;
- preparing objective personnel specifications, using only necessary and relevant criteria required to do the job;
- taking steps to ensure that vacancies reach as wide a pool of potential applicants as practicable, by considering the wording of advertisements and where they are published;
- reviewing the use of any occupational tests to ensure that they really are an appropriate and unbiased means for assessing the skills and attributes necessary for a job;
- assessing candidates against clearly identified requirements for a job to avoid making judgements on the basis of assumptions or stereotypes;
- preparing thoroughly all stages of the interview process so that candidates are assessed solely against job-related requirements;
- examining mechanisms such as application forms (what they contain, how, when and to whom they are issued) and the short-listing process;
- checking the system and criteria for identifying and selecting employees for further training;
- ensuring that all staff involved in the recruitment process are given adequate training, to reduce the risk of possible discriminatory attitudes affecting decisions and to ensure that they are conversant with the relevant provisions of the law.

It is important that a system of regular reviews is established to ensure that unlawful or unfair practices are not introduced inadvertently. Reviewing procedures help organizations to identify the areas where an equal opportunities policy is successful and those areas in which there may still be cause for concern. All employees need to be made aware of the procedures and a specific reference to them might well be included in an organization's equal opportunities policy.

Recruitment

Unless a job is covered by an exception, it is unlawful to discriminate directly or indirectly on the grounds of sex or marriage:

- in the arrangements made for deciding who should be offered a job;
- in any terms of employment;

- by refusing or omitting to offer a person employment (Section 6(1)(a); 6(1)(c)).

It is therefore recommended that:

- Each applicant should be assessed according to his or her relevant experience and professional competence. These factors, and not an applicant's gender or marital status, should form the criteria for appointment and promotion.
- Any qualifications or requirements applied to a job which effectively inhibit applications from one sex or from married people should not be retained unless they are strictly justifiable in terms of the job to be done.
- Any age limits/considerations should be retained only if they are necessary for the job. An unjustifiable age limit/consideration could constitute unlawful indirect discrimination, for example, against women who have taken time out of employment for child-rearing or against older applicants.
- Recruitment procedures should be freely available to employees and job applicants and their availability should be made known.
- A record of procedures in making individual appointments and promotions should be kept, showing, for example: the number of male and female applicants, who drew up the short-list, who was interviewed, who was on the interviewing panel. These records are useful for monitoring purposes.

Genuine Occupational Qualifications (GOQs)   It is unlawful, except for certain jobs when a person's sex is a Genuine Occupational Qualification for that job, to select candidates on the grounds of sex (Section 7(2); 7(3) and 7(4)).

There are very few instances in which jobs qualify for a GOQ on the grounds of sex. However, exceptions may arise, for example, where considerations of privacy and decency are involved. When a GOQ exists for a job, it applies also to promotion, transfer or training for that job, but cannot be used to justify a dismissal. In some instances, the GOQ will apply to some of the duties only. A GOQ will not be valid, however, where members of the appropriate sex are already employed in sufficient numbers to meet the employer's likely requirements without undue inconvenience. It is recommended that advice is sought from the EOC or CRE before acting upon the assumption that a GOQ exception applies.

Sources of recruitment   It is unlawful unless a job is covered by an exception:

- to discriminate on the grounds of sex or marriage in the arrangements made for determining who should be offered employment, whether recruiting by advertisements or by any other means;
- to imply that applications from one sex or from married people will not be considered (Section 6(1)(a));
- to instruct or put pressure on others to omit to refer for employment people of one sex or married people unless the job is covered by an exception (Sections 39 and 40).

It is also unlawful when advertising job vacancies to publish or cause to be published an advertisement which indicates or might reasonably be understood as indicating an intention to discriminate unlawfully on the grounds of sex or marriage (Section 38).

It is therefore recommended that:

- All vacancies should be advertised.
- Advertising should be carried out in such a way as to encourage applications from suitable candidates of both sexes. This can be achieved by the appropriate wording of job advertisements. Use of a job description with a sexist connotation (such as headmaster, draughtsman, milkman, postman, dinner lady, waiter/waitress, cleaning ladies) must be avoided. Even phrases such as 'Vacancy due to retirement of present headmaster' may give the impression that applications are welcome from one sex only.
- All advertising material and accompanying literature including pictorial information relating to employment or training issues should be reviewed to ensure that it avoids presenting men and women in stereotyped roles. Such stereotyping tends to perpetuate sex segregation in jobs and also leads people of the opposite sex to believe that they would be unsuccessful in applying for particular jobs.
- The placing of advertisements for vacancies, including responsibility for the wording to be used and where the post should be advertised, should not be left in the hands of one person.
- Careful consideration should be given to the description of senior management posts so as to preclude discouraging applicants of one sex. A job description can give the impression that applications will not be welcomed from people of one sex even though they may have the skills and experience for a management post (such as advertising for deputy headships which specify responsibility for 'boys' games', or advertisements for deputy headships in co-educational secondary schools which specify responsibility for 'boys' discipline' or 'girls' welfare').
- Care should be taken in the grading of comparable posts with the same description (for example, comparable heads of departments), and in

making appointments to such posts, to ensure that one sex is not disadvantaged.

- Care should similarly be taken in grading posts with different descriptions, to ensure that where a woman is doing work of equal value to a man, her work is not under-graded in relation to his. (On 1 January 1984, an important change was made to the right to equal pay by the Equal Pay (Amendment) Regulations. As a result, a woman may claim equal pay if she has good grounds for believing that her job, although different from that performed by a man, is worth the same in terms of the demands which it makes on her, for instance under such headings as effort, skill and decision making.)

Selection Methods

Applications and interviewing   It is unlawful, unless a job is covered by an exception, to discriminate on grounds of sex or marriage by refusing or deliberately omitting to offer employment (Section 6(1)(c)).

It is therefore recommended that:

- Managers should seek training in the provisions of the SDA and the implications of those provisions in relation to appointments and promotions, including the fact that it is unlawful to instruct or put pressure on others to discriminate.
- Job descriptions and selection criteria which do not favour applicants of one sex should be devised, given to all applicants, and used to short-list, frame questions and agree on whom to select.
- Applications from men and women should be processed in exactly the same way. For example, there should not be separate lists of male and female or married and single applicants. All those handling applications and conducting interviews should be trained in the avoidance of unlawful discrimination, and records of interviews should be kept, where practical, to show why applicants were or were not appointed.
- The responsibility for producing either a long-list or short-list for interviews should not rest with one individual.
- Questions on application forms or at interview should relate to the requirements of the job, relevant qualifications and relevant experience. Interviewing panels should only ask questions which are relevant to the post, and designed to fit the job descriptions and selection criteria. Questions at interview should not be different for male and female candidates. Questions about marriage plans or family intentions or childcare arrangements should not be asked, as they could be construed as showing bias against women. Applicants' sex, marital status and childcare and domestic obligations should play no part in the selection

process. Information necessary for personnel records can be collected after a job offer has been made, and should have no place on the application form or in the interview process.

- At the beginning of interviewing procedures, the Chair of the interviewing panel should remind the panel that inappropriate questions must not be asked. If, in spite of contrary advice, a member of an interviewing panel asks discriminatory questions, such questions should be immediately ruled out and repudiated by the Chair and this line of questioning should not be allowed to continue.
- The 'breadwinner' concept is not a legitimate consideration in making appointments and promotions at any level. It should be assumed that it is no more important for a man than a woman to have a job, and candidates' family circumstances are not relevant to the selection process.
- Appointment panels should not act on the assumption that women are not capable of directing the work of male colleagues or of undertaking management roles at all levels.

It is also unlawful, unless a job is covered by an exception, for employers to discriminate on the grounds of sex or marriage in the way they afford access to opportunities for promotion, transfer or training (Section 6(2)(a)).

It is therefore recommended that:

- Where an appraisal system is in operation, the assessment criteria should be examined to ensure that they are not unlawfully discriminatory, and the scheme monitored to assess how it is working in practice.
- Promotion and career development patterns should be reviewed to ensure that the traditional criteria are justifiable requirements for the jobs to be done. In some circumstances, certain criteria could amount to unlawful indirect discrimination, as they may unjustifiably affect more employees of one sex.
- Care should be taken to give due consideration to candidates with different career patterns and general experience which may have resulted from combining career and family responsibilities.
- Procedures for promotion should be adhered to on all occasions.
- Promotion should be by open competition. The practice of promoting staff solely on the grounds of the recommendation of one person, which still occurs in some organizations, should be discontinued. It is clear that in a situation where there is no open competition, and decision making is concentrated in the hands of one person, the promotion process can be thought to be abused. Staff have no means of knowing whether they are being considered properly for promotion if they are not given the

opportunity to make applications. Scope for patronage should be avoided.

- Attempts should be made to standardize the grading attached to comparable posts of responsibility. Unsystematic decisions can produce anomalies which may give rise to the possibility of sex discrimination or an equal pay claim.
- Policies and practices regarding selection for secondment courses and personal development should be examined for any unlawful direct or indirect discrimination. Where there is found to be an imbalance in the opportunities for or take-up of such courses between the sexes or between members of staff of different racial groups, the cause(s) should be identified to ensure that it is not as a result of discrimination.
- Age limits for access to training and promotion should be eliminated.

Staffing

Providing equality of opportunity in relation to future or potential staff is as important as providing equal opportunities for a current workforce. It is a significant indicator of an organization's overall commitment to combating discrimination. Staffing issues should form an integral part of all organizations' equal opportunities policies.

The following points are offered as a checklist of some of the areas to which human resource managers and trainers could pay particular attention:

- Make sure that all agreed procedures are strictly adhered to in all appointment and promotion decisions, and that no resort is ever made to informal and irregular procedures.
- Make sure that the SDA, RRA and all other equality legislation is complied with in all appointments and promotions. Don't be a party to, or ratify, any decisions about appointments and promotions unless you are satisfied that the law has been observed.
- Consider carefully the organization's selection criteria, short-listing procedures and interviewing practice. All must be free of assumptions based on sex, marital status, marital intentions and family responsibilities, and of assumptions and discriminatory language founded on racial differences. Similarly, at interviews, keep to questions about the requirements of the job. This is not the place for questions about marriage plans or family intentions.
- Look critically at the distribution of posts (particularly senior ones) in your organization between men and women and staff belonging to different racial groups.

- Is counselling and pastoral care in the organization shared by men and women?
- Are women encouraged into the full range of management roles?
- Do management actively support courses which would prepare staff for promotion as part of their in-service training? Are staff of both sexes encouraged to attend?
- Does the organization have staff with special responsibility for equal opportunities?
- When interviewing candidates for new posts or promotion, how much if any value is attached to their commitment to equal opportunities?

The Law and Equal Opportunities

Who should attend? Managers and supervisors with responsibility for staff. Equality legislation and the rights and responsibilities it confers are not restricted to senior management. From boardroom to postroom both new and experienced staff in any organization who have to deal with service calls and returns, or handle problems and complaints from internal and external customers and clients by telephone or face to face would benefit.

By the end of the training programme delegates will have:

- understood their main responsibilities under the law;
- been helped to convert the legislation into everyday messages that are meaningful to them and their work;
- had an opportunity to become familiar with specific aspects of the law that apply to their jobs, perhaps through the means of a 'question and answer' session at the end of the course.

Training programmes should aim to cover the following information as a minimum:

The laws covering sex and race discrimination and discrimination against people with disabilities are designed to outlaw discrimination and promote equal opportunities. The Sex Discrimination Act was introduced in 1975, the Race Relations Act in 1976. The first legislation to protect disabled people was introduced immediately after the Second World War and has been followed by other laws and Codes of Practice in more recent years. Employers must not discriminate against anyone on the grounds of sex or race by treating them less favourably in any aspect of employment, including recruitment, training and promotion. If they do, it is referred to as direct discrimination. Examples of direct discrimination are:

• presuming some types of work are unsuitable for women or black people, and therefore specifying in a job advertisement that the vacancy is only for a man, or only for a white person;
• asking only women candidates at interview about their domestic commitments (a good rule is to never ask a woman any questions which you would not ask a man);
• allowing male employees five weeks paid holiday and female employees three weeks.

There is a second form of unlawful discrimination, known as indirect discrimination. This occurs when a condition or requirement is imposed on everyone in the workforce, but which:

• is such that the proportion of women or the proportion of a particular racial group able to comply with it is much smaller than the number of men or white employees who can;
• the employer cannot show is justified;
• is detrimental to the individual or group concerned.

Examples of indirect discrimination include:

• Setting unnecessary height requirements for a job, such as stating that all candidates must be over six feet tall. Clearly, this is a requirement which favours more male candidates, and a much smaller number of women can comply with it.
• Selecting staff by language tests or culturally biased aptitude tests. For example, requiring English language to GCSE grade C standard when a job could be adequately performed without this qualification, or asking general knowledge questions in a selection test which are entirely to do with British culture. Clearly, a lower proportion of recently arrived immigrants or people whose first language is not English could comply with these requirements.
• Placing a job advertisement in newspapers or jobcentres in all-white catchment areas.

It is also unlawful to discriminate against men or women on the grounds of marital status, such as by:

• not recruiting married people for a job which involves being away from home;
• making only married rather than single people redundant.

It is also unlawful for employers to victimize any worker for pursuing a sex or race discrimination claim. Put simply, an employee who asserts his or her rights under one of the Acts of Parliament should not, by doing so, suffer further discrimination. Employees have the right to take a discrimination claim to an industrial tribunal regardless of how long they have been in employment in an organization. In fact, even potential employees who feel that they have been discriminated against in the recruitment process have a right to take a claim to a tribunal.

Women Returners and Women in Business

Who should attend? Human resource managers interested in developing courses or career opportunities for women returners in their localities or in their organizations. Also, women who are interested in returning to work after a career break, and women interested in reviewing or taking stock of their current career situations and obstacles to career development and who wish to look ahead to future development.

The main issues:

* male/female roles;
* setting objectives;
* management styles;
* assertiveness;
* moving up the management ladder.

By the end of the training programme delegates should be able to reflect on/initiate some or all of the following issues:

Corporate-philosophy-related issues

* What is the company philosophy regarding the employment of and development of returners? What is the genesis and rationale for it?
* How is this philosophy communicated to the line managers or recruiters?
* What specific actions are taken at the corporate level to encourage favourable perceptions of returners?
* What other actions are taken to effect the necessary attitudinal changes?
* What yardsticks have been devised to judge whether the philosophy is being effectively implemented?
* What sanctions are there for effective implementation?

- What problems have been encountered in the overall implementation of the philosophy so far? What solutions have been adopted?

Family-related issues

- What kind of health and day care facilities are available for children?
- How much flexibility is there in the number of hours worked and their timing?
- What specific provision is made to allow for illness and other contingencies (for example, caring for elderly parents)?
- What problems have been encountered in the implementation of the issues raised here? What solutions have been adopted?
- Does your organization distinguish between parental and female responsibilities in its employment practices? If so, why?

Job-related issues

- What jobs/grades/occupations do returners usually enter or are likely to enter?
- What is the pecking order of jobs/grades/occupations in the company? What numbers in each case? Pay and benefits in each case?
- How is the work organized to take account of the specific needs and disadvantages of the returners (for example, home- or tele-working, phased return to work, job sharing, flexitime, part-time work)?
- To what extent does recognition of specific needs relate to career stagnation?
- How much relative weight is put on returners' previous links with the company, their previous work experience and skills and their learning potential?
- What solutions have been implemented?

Career-related issues

- What kind of contact/training is provided for during the break?
- What kind of training or counselling do the returners receive initially?
- What methods are used in assessing initial needs?
- How far does self-assertiveness/attitude formation feature in the training programme?
- What kind of training is provided to returners beyond the induction phase?
- How far does the post-induction training focus on the needs of the job held and on developmental preparation for the next job?
- Is any training given to the line managers of the returners in relation to their effective management and development?
- Have there been any specific problems in the areas covered in this section? What solutions have been adopted?

8
Analytical Training Tools

The tools, exercises and methodology used in equal opportunities training are as varied as in any other form of training. When considering such matters it is important to remember two points:

- What are the key training issues and how might they best be incorporated into a training context?
- What previous exposure have delegates had to equality issues and to equal opportunities training? In other words, what skills and knowledge do they already possess? A role-play exercise, for example, might be a very satisfactory learning tool for trainees who have a basic awareness of equality issues but might be quite intimidating to the newcomer to equality.

These are the most common tools used in equal opportunities training:

- brainstorming
- solution focusing
- cause–effect analysis
- solution–effect analysis

Brainstorming

Brainstorming is one of the simplest and most effective methods of generating ideas to understand and solve problems quickly. It is a communal activity that has few rules. However, it is very important that what few rules there are be adhered to. Every idea is recorded, no matter how trivial or improbable it may appear.

How to brainstorm

- The group leader conducts the session. A collator writes down the ideas generated by each member of the group so that everyone can see what has been suggested. This should be done on a flipchart or whiteboard.
- The collator must make sure that the problem is written clearly at the top of the chart or board to start with.
- The leader asks each group member in turn for their idea.
- To save time, the collator must ensure that the idea is recorded concisely but in such a form that it does not lose its meaning in transcription; to prevent this happening the collator should ask the originator whether the written version is indeed what the spoken version implied.
- No comments or criticisms are allowed until all the ideas have been recorded.
- The leader continues to ask group members for further ideas until no more valid or practical solutions are forthcoming.
- Members who cannot think of ideas can pass.
- Members can use ideas already recorded as the basis to develop further suggestions; that is the reason for writing the ideas down in a clearly visible manner.
- It should be apparent that the group is 'drying-up' on ideas when several people pass and the ideas suggested are becoming less and less varied from those previously suggested or developed.

Solution focusing

When the final list has been drawn up the next stage is to choose the three most likely solutions in order of potential success. The technique for this procedure is known as A–C–R (Analyse–Categorize–Rationalize) assessment.

Analyse Examine all ideas making sure that they have been numbered sequentially in the order in which they were suggested. If this has not been done it can be done at this stage. The numbering is simply a means of identifying each suggestion quickly and concisely.

Then look for generic group headings that two or more ideas could be categorized under. For example, if the problem is an office procedure that contravenes equal opportunities it might be related to:

- the stages in the procedure itself – a need to redesign the task;
- information between people or sections is uncoordinated;
- time has not been allowed for people to check their own work.

Categorize Group every idea under the main generic heading produced at the Analyse stage. Do not try to force individual ideas under any particular headings unless they fit naturally. Create more generic groups to accommodate all ideas and resist the temptation to focus down to three groups. The more separate ideas created by brainstorming the more likely the chance that more than three generic groups will be formed. This is acceptable because if none of the first three proposed solutions are successful there is the option of employing the remaining groups as potential solutions. In the event that no solution is found then brainstorming should be carried out again but with reference to the knowledge gained from the unsuccessful ideas. Even if brainstorming fails to provide the answer directly, the learning experience can be very useful when applied to other problem-solving techniques like cause–effect and solution–effect diagrams which will be dealt with later in this section.

Rationalize This stage is used to help decide the priority order in which the categories will be applied to solve the problem. It is often helpful to use the following selection criteria for rationalization of categories:

* cost (which ideas cost least to try?)
* simplicity (which ideas can be tried and assessed easily?)
* speed (which ideas can be tried and assessed quickly?)
* practicality (which ideas can be tried and assessed without disrupting work?)

The final decision can only be taken by the group and is totally dependent upon the problem, the proposed solutions and the operating culture of the organization itself.

Cause–effect analysis

This analytical problem-solving technique is also known as a fishbone diagram or Ishikawa chart, after the Japanese professor who developed the method.

Where to use These diagrams are used where a definite, known problem exists but the cause(s) and the solution do not. For example, harassment and bullying are occurring on a frequent basis in an organization, but no one is entirely sure of the cause or of what to do about it.

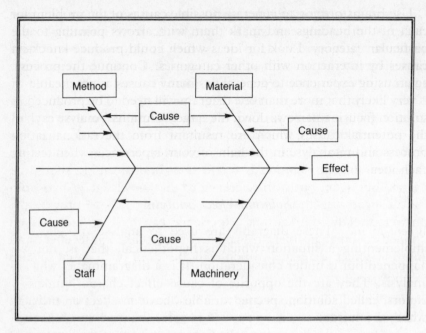

Figure 8.1 Cause–effect analysis

When to use If the solution or potential solutions to a problem cannot be identified from experience, inspection or from brainstorming because of the complicated nature of the problem or because a multiplicity of possible solutions require consideration.

How to use Cause and effect analysis, like brainstorming, is a group activity. It is advisable, especially in the early stages, for the whole group to work together on the diagram. It is best to draw up the chart on a whiteboard or flipchart so that everyone can see how the analysis is developing.

First, write the problem down in a box marked 'effect', and draw a horizontal line from the effect box outwards towards the left. Then draw four lines at a 45 degree angle to the horizontal line, two upper and two lower, and terminate them with boxes marked 'method', 'staff', 'machinery' and 'material' in any order you wish. These boxes will cover, individually or in any combination, the answer to the problem. This helps focus attention on those categories. Later, after more experience is gained in the analysis method, these boxes can be replaced with more specific, narrower categories thus shortening the time to reach solutions.

Use brainstorming to generate possible causes of the problem for each of the headings and mark them with arrows pointing to the particular category. Look for ideas which could produce knock-on causes by interaction with other categories. Continue the process, again using experience to generate as many causes as practicable. It is very likely that more than one diagram will need to be produced as solution focusing narrows down the target solutions. Analyse each of the potential causes which are resultant from the rationalization process and re-analyse in the light of your experiences when testing each idea.

Solution–effect analysis

Where to use These diagrams are used to analyse the effect of implementing a situation which is hypothetical, that is, not yet happened but is under consideration. It is a diagrammatic 'what if' analysis. They are the opposite of cause–effect charts. Numerous factors, called solution specific variables, have an effect on the outcome or solution.

When to use If the effect or potential effects of implementing a proposed solution cannot be identified from experience, inspection

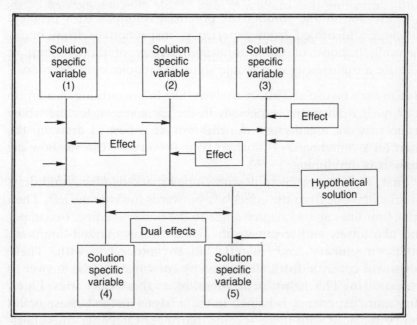

Figure 8.2 Solution–effect analysis

or from brainstorming because of the complicated nature of the problem or because a multiplicity of possible effects need to be analysed.

How to use Solution–effect analysis is another group activity. It is best to draw up the chart on a whiteboard or flipchart so that everyone can see how the analysis is developing. As with the cause and effect method it is advisable, especially in the early stages, for the whole group to work on each diagram.

First, write the proposal down in a box marked 'hypothetical solution' as shown in figure 8.2, and draw a horizontal line from the solution box outwards towards the left. Then, depending on the proposed action which is under consideration, draw vertical lines, each of which terminate in a box which is marked with a particular consideration.

Use brainstorming and experience to identify positive and negative effects under each of the main categories and to analyse possible interactions with other categories. Continue the process, to generate as many effects as practicable. It is very unlikely that one diagram will identify the yes/no decision to implement the proposed solution. Rationalize and re-analyse the resultant effects of testing and eliminating the simple and improbable effects suggested by the group.

When using solution–effect analyses it is important to be aware that there are two factors that could lead to the recommendation to implement a solution that is incorrect.

- A form of group territoriality can deceive you into wanting the effects to indicate that the solution is right. Everyone wants to see their idea implemented and it is all too easy to close the mind to categories which are negative to the solution.
- It is possible to simply miss major categories which are honestly not identified during any part of the analysis.

For these reasons use cause–effect in preference to solution–effect wherever possible. They should not be used for high-risk evaluations such as reducing staffing levels or major corporate equality studies. However, when used correctly, appropriately and with experience they are a valuable tool for equal opportunities group activities.

Sample Equality Exercises

Case studies

The use of case studies in equal opportunities courses enables delegates to focus attention on the mechanisms of prejudice and discrimination in practice. Examples are outlined below.

Case study – Anne

The scene Anne was the only female among twelve trainees in a large warehouse and removals firm. There were several hundred male workers and about a dozen women who worked part time on the administrative side.

The problem Anne came up against all sorts of problems, including sexist comments from lots of men. What bothered her most was that her colleagues were making assumptions about her which showed that their expectations of her were very low: they thought that she wouldn't be able to do the heavy lifting, wouldn't be able to get up early in the morning, wouldn't want to work in the rain, wouldn't be keen to do some jobs on her own, wouldn't want promotion, to mention just a few.

What would you have done?

1 Advised her to ignore it all and realize that 'life's like that'?
2 Helped her to assert herself in her job role and prove to her colleagues that she is just as capable of performing the job as the rest of them?
3 Talked to the rest of the workers yourself and explained why their behaviour was upsetting her?
4 Something else?

What she did Anne got the young male trainees to support her: they challenged their colleagues' sexism on her behalf. She also talked to one of the older female employees, who soon became a strong ally and source of moral support. She helped her to judge when it was best to ignore it, when to speak up and how to speak up for herself.

Case study – Susan

The scene Susan was a trainee with a large construction company. All the other employees and trainees on the construction site were male.

The problem Susan found the working environment very difficult and upsetting. She was completely ignored by the others for long stretches of time, there was no pleasant communication at all, and she experienced constant harassment, endless physical touching and continual sexist jibes. She felt very isolated, but hoped that eventually their attitude would change if she persevered long enough and proved how capable she was at her job.

What would you have done?

1 Advised her to ignore it all and realize that 'life's like that'?
2 Helped her to assert herself in her job role and prove to her colleagues that she is just as capable of performing the job as the rest of them?
3 Talked to the rest of the workers yourself and explained why their behaviour was upsetting her and that it was illegal and could be challenged under the Sex Discrimination Act?
4 Something else?

What happened Susan's approach was to keep her head down and get on with her job, a job which she was very good at. Her supervisor did notice and tried to help, but the only thing he did was to try to keep the worst offenders away from her. After a year she had enough. She quit. After several years of trying office work, which she didn't enjoy, Susan has now become a driving school instructor and is happy in her work.

Case study – Salman

The scene Salman was one of a number of trainees with a catering firm. At the time he was the company's only Asian trainee.

The problem One Monday morning, Salman's manager (who was also accountable as supervisor) told him off for being continually late. Salman flared up, having never been accused of lateness before. He told the manager he was being racist, that he was using any excuse to get at him because he wasn't white. Both of them lost all control and there was quite a slanging match.

What would you have done?

1 Brought them both together to hear both sides of the story, and make a judgement afterwards?
2 Spoken privately with the manager to say that racial issues are particularly sensitive and to be very careful about criticizing any non-white people at all?

3 Spoken with Salman to say that the manager wasn't being racist at all – the issue was lateness, and that alone.
4 Something else?

What happened Salman complained to the company director. The director investigated the complaint, first talking to Salman and the manager separately, then discussing the problem with them together. The result was that they both saw that they had each been partly to blame: Salman accepted that the manager wasn't being racist and apologized for being late; the manager apologized for being high-handed and for letting the argument get out of control in front of Salman's colleagues.

Case study – Mary

The scene Mary had stolen one record when she was fourteen. She received a fine; it was a juvenile offence. She joined a Youth Training Scheme wanting to do retail work and was placed in an ironmongers shop which was a tried and tested placement. Her scheme supervisor told the manager about the offence, with Mary's approval. No one else was told.

The problem After three weeks some tins of paint went missing. One of the female staff, Carol, had found out from a friend of her daughter's that Mary had been fined for shop-lifting. She started spreading rumours that it was Mary who had stolen the paint. Mary was very upset and confused and stated that she hadn't stolen the paint.

What would you have done?

1 Given Carol a 'talking to' and explained that there was no evidence to support her theory?
2 Told all the staff to carry on as usual and assumed it was a case of shop-lifting by a member of the public?
3 Suggested to the scheme supervisor that Mary should leave?
4 Something else?

What happened The manager confronted Mary and asked if she had stolen the paint. He explained that she could own up because even if she had, it would not mean that she would have to leave the placement; he would give her another chance. Mary continued to say that she was innocent, and was so upset that she had to leave. She said to her scheme supervisor that she thought her one offence would follow her around all her life. She was re-placed in a factory that makes ironing boards. At the factory she has been involved in printing, packing and office work and is now employed after four months as a trainee there.

Case study – Jayshree

The scene Over a period of time a supervisor noticed his Asian trainee, Jayshree, working on a gardening site, become quieter, more withdrawn and less motivated.

The problem This behaviour was untypical. The supervisor was concerned, and so kept an observant eye on her. One day he saw one of the contractors on site with her pushing and shoving her in a manner that was quite unacceptable. He called Jayshree into his office and asked if there was a problem. Jayshree explained about a whole series of incidents like the one witnessed. She had told no one.

What would you have done?

1 Tackled the contractor and told him to stop – you had witnessed what was happening and in your view it was racial harassment and was an offence under the Race Discrimination Act?
2 Phoned the contractor's company and complained to them, asking them to deal with their employee?
3 Called in outside help, such as the Race Equality Council or local union branch officer to help deal with the problem?
4 Something else?

What happened The supervisor contacted the contractor, who dismissed his employee. The supervisor counselled Jayshree that the only mistake she had made was that she hadn't said anything sooner. In fact, this case eventually went to an industrial tribunal, as the dismissed man appealed. Jayshree gave evidence and the case was upheld.

Discrimination clueword

Topics for discussion:

Tradition Many choices are based on what is traditionally expected. The group could consider examples of the different choices made by males and females because of tradition using situations appropriate to the group.

Attitudes The group could consider current approaches to attempt a change in people's attitudes towards both women and men, and try to assess their effectiveness. Suggestions of other approaches could be examined.

Commissions The Equal Opportunities Commission was set up to ensure effective enforcement of the Equal Pay and Sex Discrimination Acts. The Commission can conduct formal investigations leading to judicial hearings. The Commission for Racial Equality was set up to oversee the working of the Race Relations Act. Discuss, for example, how they can be effective for their users.

Acts The Sex Discrimination Act has been in operation since 29 December 1975. The Act makes it unlawful to treat anyone, on the grounds of their sex, less favourably than a person of the opposite sex is, or would be, treated in the same circumstances. The group could look at areas where prejudice and discrimination still exist and occur so long after 1975.

Stereotypes Examples of stereotypes could be considered – how they may have started, how inaccurate they are and the influence they have could all be discussed. Instances of specific sex stereotyping could be taken from experiences of the group.

Positive discrimination Some organizations operate a system of positive discrimination in favour of one sex which is underrepresented in a particular activity. The effects of this system as a means of achieving equality can be debated.

Family Girls and women are often discouraged from considering a long-term career because of family commitments. The traditional view of 'working husband, wife at home, two children' could be examined, as it applies to less than 5 per cent of the population.

Policy The Equal Opportunities Commission encourages organizations to draw up an equal opportunities policy, and guidelines are available to assist in this. A survey of local employers could be conducted to see how many have written policies, and copies of some of these could be examined.

Training Many courses are geared specifically towards women to encourage them back to work, to retrain in new skills and to enter areas of work dominated by men. A list of local training opportunities – and the agencies who provide information – could be made.

Equality   The group could look at areas where inequality still exists, and discuss why this should be so.

Opportunities   Courses and campaigns, such as Opportunities 2000 and the Employers Agenda on Disability, are designed to give women and disabled people a better chance of succeeding at work. Other opportunities in education and training could be investigated by the group, with discussion based on how effective they are and how their effectiveness might be improved.

Choices   At various points in a person's life, important choices must be made which will influence their future lifestyle. Times for decision making could be highlighted. Personal experiences of 'good' and 'bad' career choices made by members of an older group could, perhaps, be used as examples.

Employment   Very few jobs are restricted to a single sex. The group could look at the differences in the types of occupations entered by men and women, the reasons why this should be so and why few occupations are dominated by only one sex.

Women and men   The ratio of women to men could be looked at in terms of power – how many women are MPs, cabinet ministers, judges, company directors, barristers, top civil servants, head-teachers, surgeons, pilots, etc.? Surveys of selected areas could be carried out in small groups.

Her and him

Trainers' notes   The aims of this exercise are:

* to highlight the range of inaccuracies, assumptions and stereotypes made about women and about men and how these create barriers, build unrealistic expectations and serve to decrease equality of opportunity;
* to examine the use of language (and adjectives in particular) and its part in the promotion or discouragement of equality.

Some ideas:

Her

D   defenceless, devoted, docile, domesticated, dainty, delicate, diminutive
I   irrational, illogical, inferior, ineffective, insecure, inconsistent
S   soft, sweet, servile, subordinate, small, subservient, subjugated

C   caring, capricious, child-like, compliant, cooperative
R   romantic, refined, respectful, responsive, retiring
M   menial, meek, mild, maternal
N   nice, neat, nimble-fingered, nosey
A   abused, acquiescent, apologetic, abstracted
T   trivial, tame, tender, thoughtful, tearful, taken-for-granted, threatened, trapped
O   obedient, obscure, obsequious

Him

D   daring, distinguished, decisive, determined
I   important, independent, intrepid, immodest, intimidating
S   self-important, selfish, superior, solid, successful
C   chivalrous, courageous, competitive, cruel, conceited
R   robust, resolute, rowdy, realistic, rebellious, renowned, responsible, rugged
M   masculine, manipulative, manly, mechanically minded
N   negotiating, noisy, notorious, noteworthy
A   adventurous, achieving, arrogant, authoritative, ambitious, assured
T   talented, task-orientated, technically minded, tough
O   overbearing, overconfident, opinionated

The tutor should encourage suggestions in a spontaneous and light-hearted way. When a number of characteristics have been listed, they can be discussed by the group. Discussion could centre on:

1   whether any of the characteristics can truly be associated more with one sex than the other;
2   whether the male stereotype is credited with more positive characteristics than the female, and if so, why?
3   how such stereotyping leads to expectations which can be harmful to both sexes.

For trainees   Here are some words commonly used to describe men and women. Using the same starting letter, add other adjectives alongside:

Women are: Men are:

D   demure   D   dynamic
I   indecisive   I   influential
S   submissive   S   strong
C   coy   C   confident

R	reserved	R	rational
I	insignificant	I	independent
M	modest	M	masterful
I	illogical	I	intrepid
N	neurotic	N	noticed
A	accommodating	A	aggressive
T	timid	T	tyrannical
I	inferior	I	influential
O	obliging	O	opinionated
N	nagging	N	neglectful

Who said that?

Trainers' notes The aim of this exercise is to raise awareness of individual attitudes towards the roles of men and women in society and to examine how sex stereotyping affects work and lifestyles.

Suggested use Copies of the exercise should be handed out and completed individually. Then the answers to each remark can be compared and discussed as a group. As any of the remarks could be said by either sex, those remarks revealing a high proportion of male or female responses could be examined.

For trainees Look at the following remarks and try to imagine the speaker in each case. Indicate whether you think a woman or a man is talking by ticking under the heading; if you think the remark could be made by either, tick under the third column.

	Woman	Man	Either
1 I look after my elderly parents.			
2 I don't want a career with a lot of responsibility.			
3 When we go out, I always drive.			
4 I only work part time.			
5 I get drunk every Friday night.			
6 When I say 'No' I feel really guilty.			
7 It's not my job to clean the kitchen.			
8 I'm a systems analyst.			
9 I'll have a gin and tonic.			
10 I spend most of my salary on clothes.			
11 Dinner's ready.			

	Woman	Man	Either

12 I have to earn enough to
    support my family.

13 I run my own business.

14 No one's ever going to tie *me*
    down.

15 I'm standing as a candidate in
    the local election.

16 I stay at home these days and
    look after the children.

17 I work in an office.

18 I read the paper every day.

19 I don't like to let people down.

20 I'm at the top of my profession.

21 I got home really late last night.
    Nobody said anything.

22 I'm an eye specialist in a hospital.

23 I own my own house and car.

24 I'm the boss in this house.

25 I prefer going on holiday on my
    own.

Sex stereotyping

Trainers' notes The aims of this exercise are:

- to explain what sex stereotyping is and how it arises;
- to explore the effects of sex stereotyping;
- to encourage members of the group to be aware of their own sex-stereotyped attitudes.

Suggested use The tutor could work through the exercise with the group, bringing out discussion points which can be explored according to the awareness level of the group members.

What is sex stereotyping? Generalized comments are very often made about people – we've all heard them. When people are grouped together under one heading, this often gives rise to a single mental picture. This may not, however, be the *true* picture but it is often accepted. And this generally accepted picture then becomes a *stereotype*.

For example, think of the stereotyped picture of a Frenchman – a man with a moustache wearing a blue striped jersey and black beret with a string of onions strapped to his bicycle. Is that a true picture?

The stereotype can be totally inaccurate, without any foundation in truth. It can be extremely harmful to those being stereotyped. In the same way, women and men are often sex stereotyped. An example might be 'women like doing housework.' This is obviously not always true. The harm in this sex-stereotyped statement is that it is generally accepted that women, not men, do housework and housework is routine, unpaid, time consuming and that men would find it boring and beneath them. Examples of sex stereotyping can also be found at work, in education and in training.

Under two headings, man and woman, each group should write down the things that they associate with either a man or a woman. Later, discuss each subgroup's feelings among the whole group. By comparing lists in the group, it will become clear that men and women have set roles which lead to certain expectations. Widen the debate by focusing on how young people grow up with sex stereotyping and how they become accustomed to it. Think for instance of:

• traditional boys' and girls' toys;
• male and female sports;
• TV programmes which show sex stereotyping.

Emphasize how sex stereotyping can influence a person's choice of study, choice of career and promotion opportunities within their career, and that people who do not see beyond sex stereotyping seriously limit their own and other people's opportunities.

In the minority

Trainers' notes   The aims of this exercise are:

• to explore the local employment scene to determine the incidence of females and males in non-traditional jobs;
• to introduce the group to the experiences of women and men in these jobs;
• to encourage the group to broaden their perceptions about employment opportunities available to women and men.

(NB this exercise can be easily adapted for use with disability, age and race issues)

Suggested use   The first stage of the exercise is to involve the group in a survey of the local employment area or a large local organization to investigate occupations where one sex is still in the minority. With knowledge of the local scene, the group can suggest possible occupations, employers and organizations they wish to investigate. Local organizations such as the careers service, the Race Equality Councils, TECs and local employment action groups may also be worth approaching for further ideas and advice. Information on the numbers of females and males in specified jobs can be gathered in a number of ways including:

- by personal or telephone contact;
- by letter;
- by questionnaire;
- by collating local employment statistics.

The approach adopted by the tutor will depend on a number of factors such as:

- local circumstances;
- the chosen depth of the study;
- the existing knowledge and skills of the group;
- time and other resources at hand.

To investigate the project further, the group could split into smaller numbers to visit selected work areas or departments within their own organization. Here, they can talk not only with the women or men who are working in non-traditional jobs, but also with their work colleagues and recruitment staff. The various small group investigations could then be reported back to the main group. Alternatively, representatives of men and women working in a broad range of non-traditional occupations could be invited to speak to the group. Time should be allowed for each group to meet with both a woman and a man working in a non-typical occupation. The trainer should end this exercise by summarizing the experiences of those working in non-traditional occupations. The information gathered from the contact with those working in jobs traditionally associated with the opposite sex can be used to create a series of handouts to encourage others to widen their choice of careers.

Here are some ideas:

A man working as a . . . secretary, sewing machinist, canteen assistant, receptionist, housekeeper, nanny, model, typist, dental surgery assistant, dietitian, dancer, midwife, library assistant, florist, cleaner, room attendant, beauty therapist, care assistant, check-out cashier, nursery nurse, playgroup leader, physiotherapist, house-husband, anything else?

A woman working as a . . . window cleaner, HGV driver, Merchant Navy officer, porter, security guard, bricklayer, bank manager, union official, farm manager, pilot, oil rig worker, gamekeeper, surgeon, post-woman, MP, car salesperson, ambulance driver, funeral director, stockbroker, building surveyor, fire-fighter, golf green-keeper, gas fitter, cinema manager, anything else?

The group or a spokesperson could interview a guest speaker in a non-traditional career asking about the following:

• the reactions of their friends and relations when they first chose their jobs;
• how people react to seeing an 'unexpected' sex in the job;
• the approach they adopt if they are faced with sexist attitudes;
• relationships they have with their work colleagues;
• their advice to others of their sex considering entering the same job.

A woman's work

Trainers' notes The aim of this exercise is to raise the group's awareness of matters relating to men and women in employment.

Suggested use Members of the group should complete the exercise individually, and then the answers could lead to an open discussion.

Answers:
1 TRUE There are no restrictions on women training as civilian airline pilots. British Airways appointed its first women pilots (three) in 1987, although British Caledonian (which merged with British Airways in 1988) had employed them for several years.
2 FALSE There is no evidence to suggest that females have a stronger instinct towards childcare than males. What is certain is that girls, from a very early age, are encouraged to develop an interest in child-rearing and domestic activities, for example, with dolls, through books, TV and the media, etc.
3 TRUE Part-time employees often do not qualify for certain pension schemes and conditions of employment. This puts them in a far less secure position than full-time workers.
4 FALSE Women can work as fire-fighters provided they can pass the entrance tests under the same conditions as male applicants – these may include being able to carry a twelve-stone person a distance of 100 yards and having a 37-inch or 38-inch expanded chest measurement.

5 FALSE   There is no evidence to suggest that boys are more naturally inclined towards technical activities. They are usually given, from an early age, greater opportunity and encouragement in technical tasks than girls are.

6 TRUE   There are over 2 million people employed in engineering, and about 20 per cent of them are women. About 90 per cent of these women, however, are in secretarial/clerical jobs or semi/unskilled operative work. There are still very few women employed in technical operations.

7 TRUE   The Equal Pay Act makes it illegal for differences in pay to exist between women and men doing the same job for work of equal value.

8 FALSE   Training for midwifery is open equally to men and women. Men are called 'male midwifes'.

9 TRUE   Since November 1987, legislation has been extended to cover work on the UK continental shelf. Women in gas and oil industries account for barely 1 per cent of the workforce.

For trainees   Look at the statements below and decide whether they are true or false

	True	False
1 In 1987, only 31 of nearly 5,000 registered airline pilots in Britain were women.		
2 Females have an inbuilt propensity to look after children.		
3 Part-time workers in the United Kingdom – of which some 90 per cent are women – do not always have the same rights and provisions as full-time workers.		
4 Women cannot work for the fire service in this country.		
5 Boys are naturally suited to technical work.		
6 The majority of women employed in the British engineering industry are in administrative jobs.		
7 Under British law, men and women must be paid the same for doing the same job.		
8 Boys cannot train to become midwifes in the UK.		
9 Women can work on oil rigs.		

Quizzes – questions and answers

The aim of this exercise is to stimulate debate about the issues that fall within equality provision.

Suggested use In equal opportunities awareness raising.

Quiz number one

1 Name two areas in which the Sex Discrimination Act has forbidden discrimination.
2 What group of people is Section 28 of the Local Government Act most likely to affect?
3 What is a designated employment scheme? Name one.
4 What is meant by positive action?
5 What is the quota scheme? Which employers have to abide by it?
6 What is a spent conviction?
7 A homophobic person discriminates against whom?
8 Name two organizations from whom you can get information and assistance for offenders and ex-offenders.
9 How many types of discrimination do the Sex Discrimination Act and Race Relations Act define? What are they called?

Quiz number two

1 Which organization is chiefly responsible for overseeing the working of the Race Relations Act?
2 Is it compulsory to register as a disabled person?
3 How many people make up an industrial tribunal? What are their roles?
4 What is a stereotype? Give three examples.
5 Name three items of information that an equal opportunities policy should include.
6 Name two objectives of the European Commission's equality networks.
7 Name two organizations where you could get information on age-related issues.
8 Give an example of indirect race discrimination.
9 Give an example of indirect sex discrimination.

Quiz number three

1 What is the major difference between these two groups: Disabled Persons International and the Royal Association for Disability and Rehabilitation?
2 Name two organizations where you could get advice if you considered you had encountered discrimination.

3 What details provided on a job advertisement discriminate against older people?
4 Give two examples of potentially discriminatory questions which should not be asked during a job interview.
5 Name two techniques which might be used to monitor an equal opportunities programme.
6 Name two duties of the Commission for Racial Equality.
7 In a sentence, sum up the aim of the Opportunity 2000 campaign.
8 What is the principal aim of the Disabled Persons (Employment) Act 1944?
9 What percentage of the world's income is received by women globally?

  (a) 5 per cent
  (b) 10 per cent
  (c) 30 per cent

Answers to quiz number one

1 There are four areas: education; employment; the provision of goods, housing and services; and advertising.
2 Gays and lesbians.
3 A scheme in which entry to employment is reserved for registered disabled people. An example is the post of car park attendant.
4 Action which an organization may take to counter the effects of past discrimination.
5 A scheme whereby a quota of jobs (a percentage of the total workforce) is required to go to registered disabled people – the current quota is 3 per cent. Employers with twenty or more employees are required to comply.
6 If a person is convicted of a criminal offence and receives a sentence of not more than 2.5 years in prison, and does not commit another offence during a specified time, the conviction becomes spent or forgotten.
7 Gays and lesbians.
8 The National Association for the Care and Resettlement of Offenders (NACRO), and the Prince's Trust.
9 Three types: direct discrimination, indirect discrimination and victimization.

Answers to quiz number two

1 The Commission for Racial Equality.
2 No – registration is voluntary.
3 Three – one chairperson (legally qualified) and two lay people, one from the employer's side and one from the employee's.

4   A stereotype is a generalization about a person or group of people which is based on fiction instead of fact. Examples are the sly Jew, the macho Spaniard or the mean Scot.

5   (a) Names of personnel responsible for the policy, (b) definitions, for example, of direct discrimination, and (c) examples of unlawful action.

6   To enable the exchange of information between Member States, and to provide financial support for positive action measures.

7   Age Concern, and Help the Aged.

8   Indirect racial discrimination consists of applying a condition which nominally applies to everyone but indirectly discriminates against a particular racial group. An example is insisting that job applicants have a GCSE qualification in English language, even though it is not necessary to perform the job. Individuals whose mother tongue is not English are indirectly discriminated against.

9   Indirect sex discrimination means that conditions are applied to everyone but have the effect of placing one sex at a disadvantage. An example is insisting that job applicants are over six feet tall: a requirement which considerably more men can comply with than women.

Answers to quiz number three

1   Disabled Persons International (DPI) is run entirely by disabled people, whereas the Royal Association for Disability and Rehabilitation (RADAR) is controlled largely by non-disabled rehabilitation professionals.

2   Sources include the Equal Opportunities Commission; equal opportunities officer in the workplace; trade union representatives or shop stewards.

3   Upper age limits.

4   What child care arrangements have you made? and are you planning to get married?

5   Questionnaire, attitude survey, statistics.

6   (a) To work towards the elimination of discrimination, and (b) to promote equality of opportunity and good race relations between different racial groups.

7   To increase the quantity of women in the workforce and to enhance the quality of work they pursue by the year 2000.

8   The aim of the Disabled Persons Act is to assist people who are handicapped by a disability to gain suitable employment which will make the best use of their skills.

9   (b) 10 per cent.

Appendix 1
Address List

Advisory, Conciliation and Arbitration Service Regional Offices (ACAS)

London
Clifton House
83 Euston Road
London
NW1 2RB

Merseyside
Cressington House
249 St Mary's Road
Garston
Liverpool
L19 ONF

Midlands
Leonard House
319–323 Bradford Street
Birmingham
B5 6ET

Northern
Westgate House
Westgate Road
Newcastle upon Tyne
NE1 1TJ

North-west
Boulton House
17 Chorlton Street
Manchester
M1 3HY

Nottingham
Anderson House
Clinton Avenue
Nottingham
NG5 1AW

Scotland
Franborough House
123 Bothwell Street
Glasgow
G2 7JR

South-east
Westminster House
125 Fleet Road
Fleet
Aldershot
Hampshire
GU13 8PD

South-west
Regent House
27a Regent Street
Clifton
Bristol
BS8 4HR

Wales
Phase 1
Ty Glas Road
Llanishen
Cardiff
CF4 5PH

Yorkshire and Humberside
Commerce House
St Alban's Place
Leeds
LS2 8HH

Age Discrimination and Pre-retirement Issues

Age Concern – England
Astral House
1268 London Road
London
SW16 4ER

Age Concern – Northern Ireland
6 Lower Crescent
Belfast
BT7 1NR

Age Concern – Scotland
54A Fountainbridge
Edinburgh
EH3 9PT

Age Concern – Wales
4th Floor
1 Cathedral Road
Cardiff
CF1 9SD

FREE (Forum on the Rights of
    Elderly People to Education)
Education and Leisure Officer
Age Concern England
1268 London Road
London
SW16 4EJ

The Pre-Retirement Association
    (PRA)
19 Undine Street
London
SW17 8PP

AIDS and HIV

Body Positive (London)
51b Philbeach Gardens
London
SW5 9EB

Health Education Authority
    (HEA)
Hamilton House
Mabledon Place
London
WC1H 9TX

National AIDS Trust
14th Floor
Euston Tower
286 Euston Road
London
NW1 3DN

Positively Women
5 Sebastian Street
London
EC1V OHE

Terrence Higgins Trust
52–54 Grays Inn Road
London
WC1X 8JU

Childcare

Black Childcare Campaign
Wesley House
4 Wild Court
London
WC2B 5AU

British Association for Early
    Childhood Education
    (BAECE)
111 City View House
463 Bethnal Green Road
London
E2 9QH

Childcare Association
(of Private Nursery Providers)
8 Talbot Road
London
N6 4QR

Childcare Now
Wesley House
4 Wild Court
London
WC2B 5AU

Daycare Trust
Wesley House
4 Wild Court
London
WC2B 5AU

Family Centre Network
National Children's Bureau
8 Wakley Street
London
EC1V 7QE

Kids' Club Network
Oxford House
Derbyshire Street
London
E2 6HG

National Association of Nursery
    and Family Care (NANFC)
7 Hilary Crescent
Groby
Leicestershire
LE6 OBG

National Childminding Associ-
    ation
8 Masons Hill
Bromley
BR2 9EY

National Council of Voluntary
    Childcare Organizations
    (NCVCO)
8 Wakley Street
London
EC1V 7QE

Play Matters/National Toy
    Libraries Association
68 Churchway
London
NW1 1LT

Pre-School Playgroups Associ-
    ation (PPA)
61–63 Kings Cross Road
London
WC1X 9LL

Professional Association of
Nursery Nurses (PANN)
St James' Court
77 Friar Gate
Derby
DE1 1BT

Scottish Association of Family
Centres
Broxburn Family Centre
1–3 Henderson Place
Broxburn
EH52 6EY

Scottish Child and Family
Alliance (SCAFA)
Princes House
5 Shandwick Place
Edinburgh
EH2 4RG

Scottish Pre-School Play Association
14 Elliot Place
Glasgow
G3 8EP

Wales Pre-School Playgroups
Association
2a Chester Street
Wrexham
Clwyd
LL13 8BD

Working for Childcare
77 Holloway Road
London
N7 8JX

Working Mothers Association
77 Holloway Road
London
N7 8JX

Voluntary Organizations Liai-
son Council for Under Fives
(VOLCUF)
77 Holloway Road
London
N7 8JZ

Disability

British Council of Organiz-
ations of Disabled People
(BCODP)
St Mary's Church
Greenland Street
Woolwich
London
SE18 5AR

The Disability Alliance
25 Denmark Street
London
WC2H 8NJ

Employers' Forum on
Disability
5 Cleveland Place
London
SW1Y 6JJ

Royal Association for Disability
and Rehabilitation (RADAR)
25 Mortimer Street
London
WIN 8AB

Addresses of the Offices of Opportunities for People with Disabilities

Head Office
1 Bank Buildings
Princes Street
London
EC2R 8EU

Birmingham
The Gate House
Wellhead Lane
Birmingham
B42 3SY

Brentwood
Brentwood Community Agency
Essex Way
Brentwood
Essex
CM13 3AX

Bristol
Cadbury's Building
Somerdale
Keynsham
Bristol
BS18 2AU

Crawley
Room 3/3B Beehive Building
Gatwick Airport South
Gatwick
Crawley
RH6 OLA

Hove
SEEBOARD
Grand Avenue
Hove
East Sussex
BN3 2LS

Leicester
3rd Floor
Insurance House
125–129 Vaughan Way
Leicester
LE1 4SB

London
41 Chiswell Street
London
EC1Y 4SD

Manchester
Norweb
Hathersage Road
Manchester
M13 OEH

Sheffield
Neepsend PLC
3 Lancaster Street
Sheffield
S3 8AQ

Wirral
Quest International
Bromborough Port
Wirral
Merseyside
L62 4SU

Individuals may contact their local Placing, Assessment and Counselling Team (PACT) through local jobcentres. The PACT can also put you in touch with local Committees for the Employment of People with Disabilities (CEDPs).

Education and Training

Association for Management
   Education and Development
21 Catherine Street
London
WC2B 5JS

British Council for Commercial
   and Industrial Education
   (BACIE)
16 Park Crescent
London
WIN 4AP

Business & Technology Edu-
   cation Council (BTEC)
Central House
Upper Woburn Place
London
WCIH OHH

Department for Education
Sanctuary Buildings
Great Smith Street
London
SW1 3BT

Further Education Euro
   Network
Association of Vocational
   Colleges International
Middlesex University
White Hart Lane
Tottenham
London
N17 8HR

The Institute of Training and
   Development (ITD)
Marlow House
Institute Road
Marlow
Bucks
SL7 1BD

National Council for Vocational
   Qualifications (NCVQ)
222 Euston Road
London
NW1 2BZ

Scottish Institute of Adult and
   Continuing Education
   (SIACE)
30 Rutland Square
Edinburgh
EH1 2BW

Scottish Vocational Education
   Council (SCOTVEC)
Hanover House
24 Douglas Street
Glasgow
G2 7NQ

Training and Development
   Lead Body (TDLB)
81 Dean Street
London
WIV 5AB

Training, Enterprise and
   Education Directorate
   (TEED)
Department of Employment
Moorfoot
Sheffield
S1 4PQ

Employment

The British Council
10 Spring Gardens
London
SW1A 2BN

Business in the Community
227a City Road
London
EC1V 1LX

Commission of the European
  Communities
Jean Monnet House
8 Storey's Gate
London
SW1P 3AT

The Confederation of British
  Industry (CBI)
Centre Point
103 New Oxford Street
London
WC1A 1DU

Data Protection Registrar
Springfield House
Water Lane
Wilmslow
Cheshire
SK9 5AX

Department of Employment
Caxton House
Tothill Road
London
SW1H 9NF

Department of Trade and
  Industry (DTI)
Ashdown House
123 Victoria Street
London
SW1E 6RB

The Institute of Personnel
  Management
IPM House
Camp Road
Wimbledon
London
SW19 4UX

Scottish Business in the
  Community
Romano House
43 Station Road
Corstorphine
Edinburgh
EH12 7AF

Trades Union Congress (TUC)
Congress House
22–28 Great Russell Street
London
WC1B 3LS

Maternity, Paternity and Parental Rights

Association for Improvements
  in the Maternity Services
  (AIMS)
163 Liverpool Road
London
N1 0RF

The Maternity Alliance
15 Britannia Street
London
WC1X 9JP

National Association for
  Maternal and Child
  Welfare
46 Osnaburgh Street
London
NW1 3ND

The National Childbirth Trust
  (NCT)
Alexandra House
Oldham Terrace
London
W3 6NH

Offenders and Ex-offenders

National Association for the
  Care and Resettlement of
  Offenders (NACRO)
Head Office
169 Clapham Road
London
SW9 OPU

National Education Advisory
  Service
c/o NACRO
567A Barlow Moor Road
Chorlton
Manchester
M21 1AF

Race Relations

The Commission for Racial Equality

Head Office
Elliot House
10–12 Allington Street
London
SW1E 5EH

Yorkshire Bank Chambers (1st
  Floor)
Infirmary Street
Leeds
LS1 2JP

Regional offices
Alpha Tower (11th Floor)
Suffolk Street
Queensway
Birmingham
B1 1TT

100 Princes Street
Edinburgh
EH2 3AA

Haymarket House (4th Floor)
Haymarket Shopping Centre
Leicester
LE1 3YG

Maybrook House (5th Floor)
40 Blackfriars Street
Manchester
M3 2EG

The Race Relations Employment Advisory Service (RREAS)
(part of the Department of Employment)

London (SE and SW England)
11 Belgrave Road
London
SW1V 1RB

Birmingham (West Midlands and Wales)
14th Floor
Cumberland House
200 Broad Street
Birmingham
B15 1TA

Leeds (Yorkshire and Humberside, Northern England)
City House
New Station Street
Leeds
LS1 4JH

Manchester (North-west and Scotland)
Washington House
New Bailey Street
Manchester
M3 5ER

Nottingham (East Midlands)
Cranbrook House
Cranbrook Street
Nottingham
NG1 1EY

The Runnymede Trust
11 Princelet Street
London
E1 6QH

Sex Equality

Business and Professional Women (BPW)
Head Office
23 Ansdell Street
Kensington
London
W8 5BN

The Equality Exchange
Overseas House
Quay Street
Manchester
M3 3HN

The Equal Opportunities Commission (EOC)

Head Office
Overseas House
Quay Street
Manchester
M3 3HN

Scotland
St Andrew's House
141 West Nile Street
Glasgow
G1 2RN

Wales
Caerwys House
Windsor Lane
Cardiff
CF1 1LB

European Women's
Management Development
Network (EWMDN)
c/o European Foundation for
Management Development
Rue Washington 40
B-1050 Brussels
Belgium

National Women's Aid
Federation
374 Featherstone Street
London WC1

Opportunity 2000 (for further
information)
Business in the Community
5 Cleveland Place
London
SW1Y 6JJ

Rights of Women (ROW)
52/54 Featherstone Street
London
EC1 8RT

Women Against Sexual
Harassment (WASH)
242 Pentonville Road
London
N1 9UN

Sexual Orientation

Black Lesbian and Gay Centre
Annex B
Tottenham Town Hall
Town Hall Approach Road
London
N15 4RX

Campaign for Homosexual
Equality (CHE)
PO Box 342
London
WC1X ODU

Lesbian and Gay Employment
Rights (LAGER)
St Margaret's House
Bethnal Green
London
E2 9PL

The Stonewall Group
2 Greycoat Place
Westminster
London
SW1P 1SB

Local Organizations

The addresses and telephone numbers of these organizations can be
found in local telephone directories:

Chambers of Commerce
Citizens Advice Bureaux
Community Health Councils
European Information Centres
Health Education Unit of local
   Health Authority
Local Authority

Local community groups
Local Education Authority (LEA)
Local Enterprise Companies
Local Jobcentres
Racial Equality Councils (RECs)
Training and Enterprise Councils
   (TECs)

Appendix 2
Glossary of Terms

Advisory, Conciliation and Arbitration Service (ACAS)   The role of ACAS is to settle an employment-related dispute before it reaches an industrial tribunal. As soon as a complaint is received by a tribunal a copy is sent to an ACAS officer. The ACAS officer attempts to arbitrate between the two parties in order to reach a settlement.

Affirmative action   dates from the programme introduced in the USA by President Lyndon Johnson in 1964 prohibiting discrimination in employment. The programme requires contractors to establish measurable integration goals and timetables in order to achieve equality of opportunity.

Age discrimination or ageism   Treating people of a particular age or age group less favourably than others of a different age has become known as ageism. It is usually a bias against older people which manifests itself in prejudice and discrimination against older people. Pressure groups against ageism include the grey panthers in the USA and the growing grey power movements in the European Community.

   Images of ageism reinforce internalized attitudes of subordination and maintain practices of inequality which are mainly experienced by older women.

Arbitration   The process of resolving disputes by bringing in a third party.

Arbitrator   Person appointed by the government to help settle disputes.

Awareness raising   Gaining increased knowledge and understanding of an issue through training, group discussion and workshops. It has some similarity with the 'consciousness raising' of the 1960s and 1970s within the Women's Liberation Movement (WLM) and Gay Liberation Front (GLF). It is crucial to the development of equal opportunities within an organization, in that prejudices and stereotypes can only be challenged effectively through an appreciation of their cause and effect.

Career breaks A formal arrangement for extended absence for staff who have other commitments, with an understanding that they will return at the end of the agreed period to the same or similar job. A break might, for example, be for caring for children or elderly relatives, or for studying. It is important that during the career break staff are kept in touch with developments and issues relating to their job, for example through network meetings.

Code of practice Documents issued by the government or a governing body such as the Equal Opportunities Commission to provide guidance on a specific topic.

Collective agreement An agreement reached between management and trade unions which covers a particular working group.

Conciliation The process of resolving disputes by involving a third party who does not make a decision but tries to aid the process of reaching agreements.

Contract compliance is about attaching conditions to employment contracts to promote socially desirable ends.

Corporate strategy Assessment of the relationship between an organization and its environment (clients, customers, competitors, suppliers, domestic and international governments, etc.) resulting in a plan to achieve the business objectives.

Demographic time bomb A fairly recently coined phrase which refers to the forthcoming population changes and their effects on the labour market. By 1995 the overall workforce in the UK is predicted to increase by around 800,000, but there will be 1 million fewer 16–19 year olds. The average age of a British worker is rising. Economic recession and high unemployment may have delayed the fuse of the demographic time bomb, but the fact remains that employers will very shortly be forced to address age discrimination in their recruitment and promotion patterns, and take far more consideration of the potential of older workers if they are going to survive.

Designated employment schemes Passenger electric lift attendants and car park attendants have both been designated by the Secretary of State for Employment. This means that entry into these occupations is reserved for people on the register of disabled persons.

Disablism Discrimination against people with disabilities. It is entrenched in Western culture, in which many disabled people have had to rely on charity because of their lack of civil rights.

Discrimination Occurs when one group or individual is treated less fairly than another group, usually on the grounds of race, sex, age or disability. Double or multiple discrimination occurs when two or more discriminators, such as a person's race and sex, combine to render him or her more open to discrimination.

Equality The term incorporates several meanings. In sum, equality is based on the idea that no individual should be less equal in opportunity or in human rights than any other.

Equality clause An equality clause is a provision relating to terms of pay and other conditions of an employment contract under which a woman is employed. The Equal Pay Act 1970 (as amended by the Equal Pay (Amendment) Regulations 1983) operates by automatically inserting an equality clause directly or indirectly (that is, by means of a collective agreement) in the terms of women's employment contracts.

Equality target An equality target is a percentage of employees from an underrepresented group which an employer aims to have in the workforce by a specified date. Targets should:

- relate to the numbers or proportions of people from underrepresented groups in, or recruited to, particular jobs or grades;
- cover jobs which require higher grade skills, carry additional responsibility, or provide essential experience for longer-term career development;
- also be expressed, where appropriate, in terms of the composition of the workforce as a whole.

Evaluation means the process of checking an equal opportunities programme of activities to assess the usefulness or effectiveness of various measures. It usually follows on from monitoring, and both processes help to assess the extent to which equality objectives are being met. This provides useful feedback on the content of training and can form the basis for further development. Evaluation is a proactive process which looks to the future. It is distinct from inspection, monitoring and quality assurance, which focus primarily on measuring retrospectively whether objectives have been reached. Evaluation goes beyond that to scrutinize, and constantly review, the objectives themselves. Consequently, evaluation is concerned with the collection, analysis and interpretation of evidence in relation to a programme or policy. It requires critical judgement about a number of issues:

- the achievement of objectives,
- the efficiency and effectiveness of processes,
- the validity of initial objectives,
- the nature of unintended outcomes.

If made correctly, these critical judgements, based on the evidence collected by the evaluators, should lead to an assessment of the impact of a training programme in relation to both its objectives and its funding.

A number of general principles need to be considered when undertaking evaluation at any level:

Audience it is crucial to be aware, from the outset, of the nature and requirements of the audience.

Confidentiality much evaluation involves obtaining the views or records of individuals. Ensuring appropriate levels of confidentiality is essential to maximizing the level and integrity of responses.

Collaboration evaluation invariably requires the cooperation of many people, and calls for sensitivity to their reactions, particularly those potentially under threat from the results of the exercise.

Link to action a mechanism to feed evaluation findings into management information services is vital. Without a clear link between evaluation and action, the exercise may lead to both wasted resources and false expectations of change.

Flexible working time (FWT) Arrangements where individual employees can choose the time which they start and finish work between certain core hours. Normally there has to be a minimum number of hours worked in a given period, usually over four weeks. Flexible working also describes a range of other working practices which make it easier for employees to combine work and family responsibilities and which will also meet the needs of employers.

Genuine Occupational Qualification (GOQ) Reasons such as authenticity or decency which are allowed by law to exempt an employer from the Sex Discrimination Act and Race Relations Act.

Grey power Coined within the last decade, the term refers to the growing number of older people who are actively campaigning for more rights and for non-discrimination on the grounds of age. Also known as the grey movement, it is gaining increasing support and attention from policy makers and the general public alike.

Homophobia Prejudice and discrimination against lesbians and gay men. Like other forms of discrimination, it may be either an individual response towards homosexuality or a collective institutionalized response. An example of the latter occurs where an organization refuses to recruit or promote lesbians and gay men.

Industrial tribunals (ITs) were introduced in 1965 to solve work-related disputes and are among the least formal aspects of the British legal system. Tribunals have three members: a chairperson who must be legally qualified, and two lay people, one from the employer's side and one from the employee's side.

Integration This is one of the ideals in race relations, governing policies aimed at providing for groups of different backgrounds and beliefs to participate in society on an equal basis without losing their distinctiveness as a group. If total integration is achieved people retain their cultural identity and are accepted as equal. In the context of disability, integration is often used to describe the policies and practice of integrating young people with special learning needs into mainstream education and adults with special needs into mainstream employment.

Job sharing Two people agreeing to share one full-time job. They may work part of the day each, part of the week each or alternate weeks.

Maternity rights United Kingdom legislation provides a pregnant woman employee with four separate rights, each of which has its own qualifying rules:

1 the right to time off for ante-natal care;
2 the right to receive Statutory Maternity Pay (SMP);
3 the right to return after maternity leave;
4 the right not to be dismissed on the grounds of pregnancy.

Not every pregnant employee is entitled to all of these rights and it is therefore necessary to consider each set of rules to establish which apply to any particular employee. These rules are to be found in the

Employment Protection (Consolidation) Act 1978, and, in the case of SMP, the Social Security Act 1986.

Monitoring is the process of checking or reviewing equal opportunities policies to see if their aims are being put into practice. Monitoring methods vary: they include questionnaires, surveys, formal and informal discussions, as well as the use of statistics.

Parental leave A period of leave granted to new parents or to parents with children below school age. Under UK law there are no statutory rights to parental leave as such but a number of employers are beginning to make provision through negotiating with their employees for career breaks and other forms of family-centred working practices.

Paternity leave Like maternity leave, paternity leave refers to a period of absence from employment for fathers to care for a new baby. In the UK there are no statutory rights to paternity leave but an increasing number of employers are allowing their employees to take two or three days paid absence from work.

Positive action is a range of measures which employers and others can lawfully take to encourage and train people from a racial group or from one sex which is underrepresented to help them overcome disadvantages in competing with other applicants for new jobs, promotion or training opportunities. Measures can also be taken to help those who have a special educational or training need because of the period for which they have been carrying out domestic or family responsibilities to the exclusion of regular full-time employment. However, actual selection for interviews and jobs must be based on merit alone.

Prejudice is the thought process which can lead to discrimination. As the word suggests, prejudice is based on pre-judgements which are made without adequate knowledge. They are often based on ignorance and speculation, rather than on fact.

Quota Introduced under the Disabled Persons Act 1944, which stated that employers with twenty or more workers have a duty to employ a quota of registered disabled people (the percentage is currently 3 per cent).

Racism A combination of racial prejudice and discrimination based on the notion that whiteness is the norm and is therefore superior to blackness. Racism is usually considered to be the process whereby black people are oppressed and discriminated against by white people. It is manifested in several ways, ranging from physical violence to verbal abuse.

Register of Disabled Persons The Register of Disabled Persons was set up to help people with disabilities gain employment. Registration is voluntary but some of the facilities reserved for disabled people are reserved specifically for those who register. People eligible for registration are those who, on account of injury, disease or congenital deformity are substantially handicapped in getting employment or keeping suitable employment, and whose disability is likely to last at least twelve months. Both employed and unemployed people can apply for registration. When an individual has been assessed by a PACT officer and registered, he or she is issued with a Certificate of Registration, known as a green card, which is valid for a fixed period.

Segregation Usually the separation of groups by race in restricted areas or facilities. Occurs when individuals or groups are separated and marginalized from mainstream society. An example is racial segregation such as occurred under the apartheid system in South Africa.

Some feminists argue that women are occupationally divided into horizontal and vertical segregation. Horizontal segregation exists when men and women are working in two different sectors of a job or industry and vertical segregation exists because men tend to work at higher grade jobs and women at lower grade jobs. These forms of segregation lead to a double discrimination against many women workers.

Sexism Discrimination and prejudice based on sex, usually biased against women. Sexism is based on the notion that men are the superior sex, and has meant that men have dominated and controlled women's lives.

Sexual harassment Unacceptable behaviour which is unreasonable, unwelcome and offensive. Women are the main victims of sexual harassment and the workplace is the most likely venue in which it occurs. It is not actually defined in the Sex Discrimination Act, but since 1985 when the first successful claim of sexual harassment was made, it has been possible to claim under section 1 of the Act if less favourable treatment is received on the grounds of sex. At a tribunal a claimant has to prove that she was dismissed, forced to resign, or endured some other serious detriment as a direct result of the alleged harassment.

Statutory Maternity Pay (SMP)   was introduced from 6 April 1987. It is payable to employees who take maternity leave or leave employment because of pregnancy or confinement and who satisfy certain qualifying conditions. SMP replaced the old system of maternity provision under which women could receive maternity allowance from the state and, where applicable, maternity pay from their employers. Like statutory sick pay, where statutory maternity pay is properly paid, it can be reclaimed from the government by way of deductions from National Insurance contributions.

SMP is payable by employers to employees. For a pregnant employee to qualify for SMP she must:

1   have been continuously employed by her employer for at least 26 weeks (irrespective of the number of hours worked) ending with the 15th week before the expected week of confinement (EWC) (this 15th week is known as the Qualifying Week (QW));
2   have average weekly earnings of not less than the lower earnings limit for the payment of NI contributions which is in force during her QW;
3   still be pregnant at the 11th week before the EWC, or have already been confined;
4   have stopped working for her employer wholly or partly because of pregnancy or confinement;
5   provide her employer with notice of her maternity absence;
6   provide her employer with evidence of her EWC.

Stereotypes   are generalizations about a group of people which are often based on insufficient evidence. Caricatures of people are based on stereotypes: the mean Scot, the macho Spaniard, the fiery redhead, are examples.

Time off for family responsibilities   A period of leave granted to employees to fulfil family duties. Under UK legislation there are no statutory rights to leave for family responsibilities but a number of collective agreements permit leave for family births, deaths and occasionally for a child's illness.

Victimization   Being treated less favourably than other people because of making allegations about discrimination in good faith and asserting rights under either the Sex Discrimination Act or Race Relations Act. For example, being dismissed on the grounds of starting legal proceedings about discrimination in training provision or access to promotion.

Welfare benefits   There are three types of welfare benefits:

Non-contributory benefits   which an individual can claim because he or she is part of a group of people entitled to claim them; for example, someone who is bringing up a child on his or her own can claim child benefit.

Contributory benefits   Only if enough National Insurance (NI) contributions have been paid can someone claim one of these benefits; for example, unemployment benefit.

Means-tested benefits   These are special need payments. Whether a person is entitled to them depends on his or her income, outgoings and savings, in other words, their means. They also include housing benefit and income support.

Appendix 3
Laws

1992 The Further and Higher Education Act
1994 Age of Consent Law reform

European Union law – an outline

Outlined below are summaries of the different types of European Union measures in use. These are:

Directives A Directive is a European Union law which is legally binding on all Member States. In most cases this means that national legislation has to be proposed or current laws have to be changed in order that they comply with the Directive's requirements.

Regulations A Regulation is a law which is binding on all Member States but does not require any national legislation to be implemented.

Decisions Decisions can be issued either by the Council of Ministers or by the European Commission. They are legally binding on those to whom they are addressed. They may be addressed either to a Member State, a company or to an individual.

Recommendations and Opinions Neither Recommendations nor Opinions have any legally binding effect. They are not laws. Instead, they state the view of the institution that issues them (in general, the European Commission) and they may encourage or suggest that certain action be taken.

Appendix 4
Costing Training: Costing Formulae

A basic way of costing or budgeting for training is to divide the trainer days into cost of the training service or unit. This can also be applied to situations where there is no unit, only one person.

Making financial decisions about training involves considering a number of key issues. Two essential questions to consider are:

- How many people require training?
- Where is the training going to take place?

Answering these two questions enables decisions to be made about other issues, for example:

1 Is an in-house equal opportunities trainer, such as the human resource manager, available and capable of doing the training?
2 Do we require an external trainer? If so, who?
3 Are we budgeting on a per participant per day basis?
4 Opportunity costs.
5 Cost breakdown.

Breaking down costs is usually done in either of the following ways:

1 Cost per participant is calculated as a percentage of the overall cost along lines such as 20 per cent overheads, including staff salary, preparation, planning, administration; 80 per cent costed per participant per day, and this includes cost of outside trainers, evaluation, planning, accommodation. This method can be arbitrary and hide the true costs of some of the activities.
2 The training process is segmented, as are all the activities involved, and each is costed separately to give the overall cost, which is then divided the way the organization requires.

Key points to consider

- Have you made any attempt to cost your training activities?
- What methods does your organization use to cost training?
- Where could you get information on costing training?
- What differences does it make to the costing task if you view the organization/department, rather than the participants, as the client?
- Do you have a training budget? or, have you explored ways of gaining more financial control?
- What financial help may be available, either locally or through European funding?
- Do you have access to other resources, not just financial ones, that may well reduce the costs inherent in transport, loans of equipment, supply of stationery?

Index

INDUSTRIAL RELATIONS JOURNAL

Edited by Brian Towers

The **Industrial Relations Journal** is a leading international journal for industrial relations, employee relations and human resource management practitioners, policy-makers and academics. It monitors, reports and predicts significant developments in these areas. The annual subscription includes four issues of **IRJ** plus two companion issues of **New Technology, Work and Employment. NTWE** is concerned with all aspects of modern work and employment, especially relating to the impact of new technology.

Recent and forthcoming articles include:

Industrial relations and the construction of the Channel Tunnel
John Fisher

The emergence of the Euro-company: towards a European industrial relations?
Paul Marginson et al

Japan in Wales: a new IR
Barry Wilkinson et al

Does trade unionism have a future in Russia
Peter Fairbrother et al

ORDER FORM

INDUSTRIAL RELATIONS JOURNAL

Subscription Rates, Volume 25, 1994

ISSN 0019-8692

**Individuals £77.00 UK/Europe, £146.00 N America*, £98.00 Rest of World
Institutions £103.00 UK/Europe, £195.00 N America*, £131.00 Rest of World**

Published quarterly   *Canadian customers please add 7% GST

☐ Please enter my subscription/send me a sample copy

☐ I enclose a cheque/money order payable to Basil Blackwell

☐ Plase charge my American Express/Diners Club/Mastercard/Visa account number

_____ Expiry Date_____

Signature _____ Date_____

Name _____

Address _____

_____

_____ Postcode _____

E-Mail Address: jnlsamples @ cix. compulink.co.uk (Please include the name of the journal)

Payment must accompany orders
Please return this form to: Joumals Marketing, Blackwell Publishers, 108 Cowley Road, Oxford, OX4 1JF, England. Or to: Joumals Marketing, IRJ, Blackwell Publishers, 238 Main Street, Cambridge, MA 02142, USA

Blackwell Publishers   Oxford, UK and Cambridge, USA